CULTURE OF
THE FORK

ARTS AND TRADITIONS OF THE TABLE

ARTS AND TRADITIONS OF THE TABLE

Perspectives on Culinary History

Albert Sonnenfeld, series editor

Salt: Grain of Life

Pierre Laszlo

TRANSLATED BY MARY BETH MADER

CULTURE OF THE FORK

A Brief History of Food in Europe

GIOVANNI REBORA

TRANSLATED BY ALBERT SONNENFELD

COLUMBIA UNIVERSITY PRESS

NEW YORK

COLUMBIA UNIVERSITY PRESS

Publishers Since 1893

New York   Chichester, West Sussex

Translation © Columbia University Press 2001.
La civiltà della forchetta © 1998 Gius. Laterza & Figli Spa,
Roma-Bari. English language edition arranged through the
mediation of Eulama Literary Agency.

Library of Congress Cataloging-in-Publication Data

Culture of the fork : a brief history of food in Europe /
by Giovanni Rebora ; translated by Albert Sonnenfeld.

p. cm.

Includes bibliographical references and index.

ISBN 0–231–12150–4 (cloth)

1. Gastronomy. 2. Food habits—Europe.

3. Cookery, European.

TX641 .C535 2001

394.1'094—dc21   2001032450

Casebound editions of Columbia University Press books
are printed on permanent and durable acid-free paper.

Printed in the United States of America

Designed by Linda Secondari

c 10 9 8 7 6 5 4 3 2 1

CONTENTS

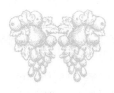

CONTENTS

CONTENTS

As translator from the Italian of this savory of culinary history, I was faced with sixty specifically named Italian words for pork or beef sausage and in English found only *sausage* and *salami*. An infinity of constellations of untranslatable pasta shapes further impeded my Promethean climb. My recompense was a keener historical awareness and appreciation of the gastronomic bounty of Bella Italia.

As series editor of Arts and Traditions of the Table, I am delighted to share this readable, insightful, and delightful history by Giovanni Rebora with a broad readership of nonspecialist food-lovers, gourmets, gourmands, and Italophiles.

I had always been convinced that frequent famines marked Europe's Early Modern or postmedieval period. In fact, for centuries, the average Italian peasant had several pounds of meat available to him each week at very modest cost. Why? Because the demand for calfskin and ox- and cowhides for saddles, wineskins, riding gear, and so on, greatly exceeded the supply. So to meet this demand, more and more cattle were bred, creating an oversupply of meat and lowering its price, but also inflating the cost of feed and pastureland.

The Catholic Church's rigid enforcement of "lean [meatless] days" added to the meat surplus, while fish and other authorized foods escalated in price. Cattle went to market on its own legs; fish had to be transported, and quickly, to avoid spoilage. Large fish were caught on line, not in nets, and were too expensive for any but the nobility and merchants.

To those who thought the fork an invention of Renaissance nobility to ensure courtly manners, I say, "Think again!"

Among the fascinating array of revealing insights dispensed by Giovanni Rebora in this readable, concise, chatty book is documentation that the single prong or spit evolved into a utensil resembling our modern fork (or digits of the diner's hand) for very practical reasons. As the Euclidean geometry of pasta shapes developed (and that was long before Marco Polo's famous voyage to China), the slippery strings of spaghettini either burned or slipped elusively through the diners' fingers. Hence the ingenious fork, which allowed one both to spear and to twirl.

Later, in some devout circles, the fork was considered a decadent extravagance or an excess of precious refinement. Even in 2001, the great three-star Milanese chef Gualtiero Marchesi is hard at work developing a new model for a pasta fork.

In keeping with his belief that practical economic needs motivate gastronomic progress and culinary technology, Rebora reminds us that plates were a creation of the Early Modern. What began as a slab of bread onto which portions of victuals were placed (the first pizza, one might say!) became, thanks to renewal of ceramics neglected since the Roman Empire, an autonomous plate. And of course pizza and the pitta of the eastern Mediterranean are etymologically and culinarily twin solutions to the same problem of how to serve food at the table.

Every chapter of this informal rendering of culinary history (and the chapters are delightfully concise) yields new perspectives on foods, class structures, topography, manners, gastropolitics and market conditions in postmedieval Europe, from south to north, with a strong Mediterranean emphasis.

From what we call the "Early Modern" to the Modern is but a step, and Giovanni Rebora guides us with a steady and friendly hand from past to present.

ALBERT SONNENFELD

INTRODUCTION

The Early Modern era begins at the end of the fifteenth century. We historians always say this, in respectful tribute to academic convention. But however arbitrary such generalizations may be, the fall of Constantinople to Mohammed II on May 29, 1453, signaled the end of a world.

The "discovery" of America on October 12, 1492, only a few months after the Christian "reconquest" of Granada (in April) and the expulsion of the last Islamic king from the Iberian Peninsula, was another memorable event, one that also marked the beginning (albeit with many delays) of a new era in culinary history, whether in Europe, America, Africa, or Asia.

Meanwhile, in Great Britain, the end of the Hundred Years' War (fought on French soil) and the end of the War of the Roses allowed the island kingdom to structure itself politically, free at last of longstanding ties to the Continental landmass.

In France, Burgundy (long allied with the English against the ragtag armies of Joan of Arc) lost its independence with the reign of Charles the Bold. But the count of Flanders, adorned with the Order of the Golden Fleece, continued the somewhat archaic splendor of the waning Middle Ages: a little of this culture survived in the Piedmont, in the dukedom of Saluzzo.

The heir to the thrones of Castille, Aragon, and Navarre, Charles I of Hapsburg, later to become Emperor Charles V, was born in Flanders. So a little of Flemish culture migrated to Spain and vice versa: flamenco survived in Andalusia, the bodegas in Flanders.

If Venice ultimately expended far too much energy and treasure defending its colonial possessions in Greece, Genoa, sagely and in stark contrast, very slowly withdrew its investments from the Orient without resorting to ruinously expensive wars. The Genoese went to Andalusia and the former Kingdom of Granada to take over from the Arabs and Jews who had been chased out by the hostile policies imposed following the Reconquest. They were solidly ensconced in Seville, as well as in the Kingdom of Granada, by the middle of the thirteenth century, and at the end of the fifteenth, of the 500 merchants in Seville, the 350 richest were from Genoa.

In Italy, in the fifteenth century, there developed the splendid cultural transformations we call the Renaissance. With the exception of the Kingdom of Naples, the Trentino, the Piedmont near Turin, and the duchy of Saluzzo (and perhaps a few tiny enclaves like the duchy of Finale), Italy was governed by Italian lords and princes, by Italian oligarchies as in Venice, Genoa, and Lucca, or else by the pope, who passed out fiefdoms to his nephews. All these lords, who were often mercenary captains of noble extraction but also bankers and merchants (in addition to the aforementioned papal relatives), enjoyed fabulous wealth. Moreover, these moneyed classes, thanks to arranged marriages with Italian and foreign nobility or perhaps in return for generous loans made to royalty, often acquired noble and feudal titles.

These nouveaux riches did not belong to the ancient nobility of Germanic stock and chose to give up Gothic

FIGURE I
Kitchen interior, eighteenth-century engraving.

forms and traditions in favor of of forms and rituals inspired by a far more ancient nobility, that of the Roman Empire. This phenomenon, which has inspired thousands of pages, produced what we call the Renaissance. More important for the story here, it also initiated a way of eating that differed radically from medieval traditions.

An essential if somewhat older tie to the Renaissance is what is called humanism. Bartolomeo Platina, a humanist, had transcribed into Latin recipes by Maestro Martino (a cook and writer) and others drawn from books written in the vernacular. His book itself had no practical utility, but the translation conferred literary dignity to the contents. It was not the first book comprising translations from the vernacular into Latin, but represents a humanistic undertaking that offers a compendium of the final phase in medieval cuisine, some of which endured in popular culinary practice until products from the New World arrived on the scene.

The very short introductory notes to a brief history of food that follow pertain above all to structures (that is, the people) and phenomena of continuing, long-term duration. Yet the economics and anthropology of food also respond to major political happenings, changes in the territorial order of regimes, great discoveries, the outcomes of wars, the triumphs and defeats of countries, and to the commercial agreements that a real and autonomous social class—that of international tradesmen—succeeded in formulating and implementing despite the frequent wars and religious differences that divided Europe, especially during what I shall call the Early Modern period.

Tradesmen exchanged more than goods and money: they also swapped ideas and above all experienced reciprocal trends, habits, and customs, including ways of cooking. Living far from their homelands for years on end, they took with them servants and cooks, and when they returned home, these servants and cooks had learned many things. Some even stayed on in the host city to practice their art.

I know that when we speak generically of that past we think of it as a long period of endemic hunger. But we need to remember that a starving man cannot work, especially if he has to climb the scaffolding of a Renaissance building site, row on a galley, or navigate by sail. I shall focus here on the tensions between the available resources and consumers' economically determined possibilities for selective choice, the rich having such a choice and the poor making do as best they could. Fear of hunger ran through Europe and often became reality. I believe, however, that food resources, measured against the size of the population, were not as scarce as is often claimed. I believe that the people mostly had at their disposal adequate food, produce, and goods. Thus the unhappiness of those who didn't have enough money perhaps did not derive from their lack of basic necessities but from the impossibility of their obtaining more than subsistence nourishment. The poor yearned for what I call "the superfluous."

Fork

CULTURE OF
THE FORK

FIGURE 2

The Baker, engraving by Giovanni Volpato, after
Francesco Magiotto, end of the eighteenth century.
(Milan, A. Bertarelli Municipal Print Collection)

CHAPTER ONE

Grain and Bread

The sixteenth century saw a remarkable growth in the European population. Obviously, there were differing rates of increase, and along with the phenomenon of urbanization itself, these variables had important consequences for the feeding of city dwellers.

Naples doubled its population (from 200,000 to 400,000 inhabitants) between the sixteenth and seventeenth centuries. London experienced the incorporation of country dwellers, who became the object of well-known ordinances for the poor (which in practice were ordinances against them).

The concentration of the rural population in the capital cities was an indication of economic decline (for the poor, naturally). The closing of fields and pastureland in Great Britain excluded many from the possibility of feeding their livestock and gathering firewood and fruits in the forests. The soil became less and less fertile. People moved to the cities.

In the Kingdom of Naples the population gravitated to the capital, and assuring supplies of the usual basic foodstuffs became ever more difficult. Emilio Sereni tells how the

Neapolitans—the "leaf eaters," as the Sicilians used to call them—became "macaroni eaters." From dishes of meat and greens the move was to pasta, which would lead, in Naples at least, to an entirely new form of eating.

The history of food, a discipline not as yet highly developed, in the past mostly investigated the wholesale business and commerce of the major foodstuffs. With this methodology one could divide the quantity of grain harvested (which is not the same thing as the real quantity) by the number of inhabitants (similarly "harvested") and derive from these statistics a certain quantity of grain: the presumed consumption per statistical unit of population.

Aside from the possible presence of breast-fed babies who should have been excluded from such statistical tallies, people are not just statistical units: they don't eat wheat "by the grain." Historians thus reasoned that since grain is transformed into bread, the official price per loaf or weight should be quoted in relation to daily salaries. This led to the conclusion that the poor statistical units stuffed themselves with eight kilos of bread per day. The notion that with grain one can produce flour, from which pasta can be made by hand, seems to have occurred to almost no one, not even when confronted with evidence of imports of hard grain destined for the fabrication of dried pasta in a pasta cutter.

The same pattern held for foodstuffs such as meat and other products. The problem lay not in food itself but in the economics of marketing food products. Men have for millennia devoted most of their time to procuring food for themselves and to preparing it.

Simply to dignify the subject of culinary history or to affirm its importance no longer suffices. Basically, eating is not an art, not a literature, not even a science. How can one study a function so basic, so necessary? I seek here first of all to discover those aspects of food tied to the notion of the "the superfluous." Doing so opens a window on the history and anthropology of food. Both cuisine and the banquet are forms of communication!

The fact remains that grain is not eaten "by the grain." Grain needs to be ground, to be brought to a publicly or privately owned mill, where the miller earns his salary or a profit intended to pay him for his labor (and that of his helpers), along with a return for his investment and the upkeep of the machines. Then there are the baker's salary and the costs of maintaining the oven (if it is a public oven). If the oven is private, you have to pay for the laborer as well as for firewood and upkeep. And there is always the tax surcharge for the Government and for rental of the premises.

Since bread belongs to the foods that in the Roman era were regulated by state allocation (the famous Annona), bread was (and still is today, albeit with obvious differences) a regulated product considered indispensable for the feeding of the people. The state was therefore compelled to involve itself by setting the price of bread and ensuring that there were no shortages, if necessary by buying grain and controlling its distribution.

Sifter

Whatever economists, especially those tending toward macroeconomics, may think, the people fed themselves on cooked foods prepared and combined as the occasion and company warranted according to an alchemical process that we call *cuisine*. These foods gradually became known dishes that were both the sum of the separate ingredients and an integration of these ingredients.

This could all be expressed in mathematical terms. The sum of the ingredients becomes something more than a sum, thanks to the balance of the parts, to the time and method of cooking, to the addition of salt or of fats, and to the action of heat. A dish composed of inexpensive ingredients can be far more complete and nutritious than the sum of those parts ingested separately.

Of all the foodstuffs bread was, in the Roman era, by far the most widely diffused, and it became the very symbol of food. In the towns bread had to be distributed in standardized configurations to which corresponded a price set by the regulators or by the relevant lawmakers. Among the peasants bread was made at home and baked in either the family or the village ovens.

One could treat oneself to white bread made of sifted wheat flour (especially in the towns) or to black or brown bread made of a blend of various cereal flours (rye, barley, spelt, etc.) or of unsifted wheat when in adequate supply. White bread, baked daily, was intended above all for whoever could pay its price; it existed in various shapes and could be seasoned with oil, lard, milk, or other seasonings.

We need to remember that Italy, even in the early modern era, was spangled with innumerable cities big and small, governed by lords and oligarchies but all linked by communal and local traditions that even the worst princes had to reckon with. The peasants constituted the largest segment of the population and lived on the land according to agreements that varied from region to region. These contracts were certainly not favorable to the toil-weary poor, but the existence of so many cities provided a source of demand and therefore a stimulus to production. Think of small family farms whose products were not intended for a single center, a capital of the kingdom, but for tens and hundreds of small regional capitals, for the tens of more or less independent

FIGURE 3

Baker, engraving from Diderot and D'Alembert, *Encyclopédie; ou, Dictionnaire raisonné des sciences, des arts et des métiers* (The Encyclopedia; or, Dictionary of sciences, arts, and trades) (Paris, 1772).

FIGURE 4

Breadseller, engraving from *Arte per via* (Bologna, 1660).

courts scattered throughout the peninsula, and for hundreds of abbeys, monasteries, and convents.

The agricultural contracts in Tuscany or Liguria indicate a substantial presence of nobility with merchant origins among the landowners. In countries outside Italy or in regions with a heavy feudal presence the contractual arrangements seem different, with a greater use of workmen, for example, than was usually agreed to in either Liguria or Tuscany.

Ownership of land by those cultivating the soil was frequent both in Liguria and in Monferrato. Inevitably, this led to the fragmentation of the property itself, which resulted in turn in smaller family farms that soon became incapable of producing revenue sufficient to sustain the farm families themselves. From this came urbanization and an indebtedness that would have consequences for the quality of such products as wine, as well as creating easy hunting grounds for those who, having lent money guaranteed by a mortgage, now demanded the land as payment.

Despite various quasi-legal strategies it proved impossible to keep farms intact. With the first succession came a division into halves (if there were two male heirs), and at the second succession each half was again subdivided.

The indebtedness of the small landowners and the grim conditions of life led to a new phenomenon: litigiousness on matters of property lines and possible profits, on rights of way and water rights, conflicts that afflicted then as now many agricultural regions. From all this arose serious difficulties, among them the abandonment of the land and poverty.

Conditions for nonlandowning peasants were hardly better: owners asked for almost everything and in the majority of cases gave nothing in return. Poor folk were badly nourished, dependent on polenta (made of spelt, beans, chickpeas). Only rarely did they eat bread, and then a bread that was almost never made of wheat.

The shortage of bread was, however, a problem that was

above all urban. Each peasant was granted a kitchen garden, a strip of land along the far limits of the fields, as well as some farmyard animals and the use of different cereals from the grain harvest. The city dweller, in contrast, had to buy everything, and bread was the symbol of his life. It is no accident that the locution "to earn one's bread" has been used for so long to indicate the price of labor.

When Manzoni described the riots in Milan shortly before the plagues of 1630, he told of an "attack on the ovens by the crippled." An attack on an oven might seem quite strange. One would expect that people intent on rebellion and pillage would head toward shops that offered foods less ordinary and more expensive than bread, at least for the poor. But this attack is fraught with symbolism: if the people are hungry, the people want bread. The rulers of the ancient republics knew this well. The people want the superfluous, to be sure, but one needs first to guarantee them the necessities. If there is a bread shortage, the people rebel and create serious problems for those in power. A shortage of the superfluous, on the other hand, makes for unhappiness but does not justify subversion.

The famine that struck Sicily during that same era is well documented. Most revealing is a letter, preserved in the State Archives in Palermo, that recounts how two victims of starvation were found stretched out on the beach with grass in their mouths. This image really hit me, and from that letter sprang my interest in the history of food. The sea at Ficarazzi would have offered to any and all a quantity of food sufficient for survival, but without bread you die. A few years later, I found the same phrase in a book by G. Doria dealing with Montaldeo. He too mentions two men who starved to death with grass in their mouths. It might be mere coincidence, but I believe that this is rather a repeated, almost paradigmatic image invoked to show the seriousness of a moment in culinary history.

If in the cities bread had to be guaranteed to the people, the use of grains and greens in diverse forms of bread allowed the rural populations to survive. And thanks to demographic pressures far less extreme than those facing urban populations, the peasants did survive and in a fashion less awful than we have been led to believe.

Sacks for transporting flour

FIGURE 5
Processing pasta, engraving from Bartolomeo Scappi,
Opera dell'arte del cucinare (Works from the art of cooking)
(Venice, 1570).

CHAPTER TWO

Soup with Bread, Polenta, Vegetable Stew, and Pasta

The recipe: take lots of water; cabbage, turnips, and other greens; a light fry of lard (or oil) and onions, garlic, and salt. If available, add a piece of salt pork or of beef (the *cecina* of the Iberian Peninsula or the Turks' *pastermé*). In season, mutton or ox bones can replace the salted meat. On the stock drawn from the long cooking process float some hard, stale bread. We Italians still talk about "bathing a soup" and "souping up the bread." This was tripe soup, made whenever conditions allowed; at other times, it was turnip or cabbage soup. The stale black bread crumbles up in the soup and begins to look like couscous.

When slaughtering time came for the pigs, one boiled up those parts that could not be salted or otherwise preserved. By adding ribs and a piece of fresh sausage, some turnips (which might replace potatoes), and cabbage, one could produce a "soup" that in Lombardy is called *cassoela*. With the mythification and ennobling of paupers' cuisine, this concoction has inspired rivers of words studded with fatuous adjectives from many a gastronome. Called a pork boil in the Benevento region, this pork-and-cabbage broth, with the addition of a few bones, could soak up a lot of stale bread.

The bread was stale because it was baked (or brought to be baked) only once a week. In the mountains it lasted even longer and was prepared with wheat and rye. The bread hardened to the point that one needed a special implement to cut it: a kind of slicer made of wood and iron that resembled a paper cutter.

If into the *cassoela* pot you threw pork ribs, bones, and other parts of the pig, beef went into other stews, such as the French *pot-au-feu*, the Spanish *olla podrida*, and the Neapolitan *pignatta maritata*. Despite the backers of various theories of indigenous culinary inventions, it was always the same soup or stew.

The need to add fats and carbohydrates (grains) to soup is universal, national or regional. In northern Europe you did it with rye or barley bread, or else you made a soup of grains or vegetables (barley, wheat, spelt, lentils, etc.) to which were added lightly fried foods and whenever possible a ham bone or some salted pork. Where bread was more widely available one prepared little pellets of flavored bread, which were then cooked in the broth. To sum up, it was usual to prepare foods that would contain fats and grains. Onions, garlic, or leeks added flavoring and the necessary fibers to the concoctions.

Fork

In the Mediterranean basin, where the quality and quantity of different greens offered a greater choice of better-quality produce, there were, to be sure, some locally idiosyncratic dishes with slightly different ingredients, but even these adhered substantially to the basic principal components of the soups.

To the east the Arabs used a hard grain, ground in a way that today would seem coarse, from which they derived a bran pasta, couscous. This they "bathed" in a soup made of herbs and roots cut into comparatively large pieces flavored with oil and pieces of mutton. Even today couscous is prepared in special tiered clay saucepans: vegetables and the mutton are cooked on the lower level; the semolina is steamed on the perforated top.

In North Africa, couscous took the name *kuskussù*. To prepare the dish you worked the moistened semolina in your hands to shape both large pellets (3 mm in diameter) and tiny grains (1 mm). *Kuskussù* spread through the western Mediterranean Tyrrhenian Sea thanks to the coral fishermen living on the island of Tabarca across the water from Tunisia who originally had come from the Genoa region (Sestri-Multedo-Pegli). The itinerary of this pasta followed the wanderings of these coral fishermen: from Tabarca toward Sardinia (where the men of Tabarca settled in 1720), toward Spain (New Tabarca) and back toward the land of their origin, Liguria.

In Sardinia *kuskussù* is called *soccu*. The tiny pellets are formed by the palms of the hands pressing the wet flour against the bottom of a basin. The coral fishermen from Alassio and the Cervo who fished at the Bocche di Bonifacio brought the food to western Liguria under the name *succu*. In Calasetta and Carloforte (settled by the Genoese from Tabarca) it is called *cascà*, and in Toulon *courcoussou* as early as 1630.

Jean-Louis Flandrin informs us that "in 1630 the Parisian Jean-Jacques Bouchard studied the Provençals' eating habits, reporting that they added pasta to their soup as in Italy: 'Moreover, in Toulon, I ate some of a kind made with small rice-like grains that swell up greatly during cooking and that they call *courcoussou*.'"

Always with a base of hard-grained bran, *kuskussù* was produced in Genoa by cutting thick preshaped spaghetti into small cylinders. But the pressures of commercial distribution ultimately led to production of a pasta that was no longer homemade but industrial.

Distorted by the local dialect, as happened with *soccu*, the name *kuskussù* became known as *scuccusù* in Genoa. This pasta ended up in vegetable soup, just as it had when it was called *kuskussù* in Tabarca and Tunisia. Whether in Liguria, Sardinia, or Spain, pasta even today is still added to soup throughout the Mediterranean (Sicily, home of the coral fishermen from Trapani, comes to mind). All these extensive migrations of *kuskussù* took place between the first half of the sixteenth and the end of the eighteenth centuries. Minestrone, flavored or not with leg of lamb, is a descendant of *kuskussù*, especially when pasta is added.

The genesis of all these traditions dates from long ago, but to the student of culinary history the birth certificates of a particular dish are mere collector's items. What really matters is the breadth of a food's spread into new territories. To be old may to be noble, but what should matter is that a food be good, nourishing, and available.

The Early Modern era, beginning with the first decades of the sixteenth century, brought an attenuated tendency toward change in customs and a slow turn toward new ways of eating. The discovery of America, along with the opening of routes to the East Indies by the Portuguese, made a major contribution, as I shall show. For now, however, let me conclude this chapter with some remarks on the ways of eating pasta and pasta's influence on table manners, beginning with the use of the fork.

The spread of the use of the fork seems tied to the spread of pasta consumption. First-hand proof of this appears in a cookbook compiled at the Angevin court in Naples and presented, in Latin translation, to King Robert of Anjou:

FIGURES 6 AND 7

Portrait of Antonio Latini and frontispiece of his work *Lo scalco alla moderna, overo l'arte di ben disporre i conviti* (The Modern Steward; or, The true art of taking care of guests) (Naples, 1694). (Rome, Collection of the Casanatense Library)

FIGURES 8 AND 9

Frontispiece and portrait of Bartolomeo Scappi, from *Opera dell'arte del cucinare* (Works from the art of cooking) (Venice, 1570).

On Lasagna: for lasagna take fermented dough and roll into a hollow tortellini shape as tightly as you can. Then divide the dough into four squares measured and shaped by the fingers. Afterward you have salted boiling water and into which you put the aforementioned lasagnas to cook. And when they have been thoroughly cooked you add grated cheese.

If you so desire you can add quality powdered spices and sprinkle these over the mixture. Then you make a serving of lasagna and this concoction and serve until the bowl is full. Then eat picking up the lasagna with a single-pronged wooden utensil (*punteruolo*).

This is the first mention of a utensil functioning like a fork, intended to "pick up" food, and also the first linkage of the utensil with pasta. The lasagne are limp and slippery; picking them up with a fork is inconvenient and awkward. Still, the recipe book from the court of Naples intended for the library of Robert of Anjou advises using a pointed prong. In bourgeois circles, where pasta had extraordinary success, a fork soon replaced the *punteruolo*.

On the spread of pasta, on the introduction of dry pasta, first in the Middle Ages and then again in the seventeenth century, I believe it useful to read the fine pages on the subject written by Massimo Montanari. Use of the fork accompanied the spread of pasta, and in fact it seems limited, from the Middle Ages until at least the end of the second half of the sixteenth century, to those areas where pasta was eaten. In the inventories of well-known castles only slightly removed from the immediate Mediterranean cultural sphere (such as the castle of Challant in Val D'Aosta) one can find gold and silver spoons and knives but not a single fork!

For Fernand Braudel, the fork "dates from the sixteenth century and originating in Venice was adopted, very slowly, through Italy and perhaps Spain. . . . Use of the fork did not become generally widespread before 1750. . . . Montaigne hadn't heard of it. . . . Felix Platter mentions the fork soon thereafter in Basel around 1590. . . . An English traveler in 1608 discovered it in Italy."

For Jean-Louis Flandrin, "the utensil was invented in Byzantium and introduced to Italian tables in the fourteenth and fifteenth centuries, after which it migrated into neighboring countries during the sixteenth and seventeenth centuries."

For some of the clergy of the time, use of the fork was a shocking overrefinement. The prelates roundly chastised a Byzantine princess who, while a guest in France, picked up her food with a fork. For her, to the royalty born, it was simply a question of good Byzantine manners not to touch food with her hands. The Ligurian, Tuscan, and Venetian burghers of the fourteenth century, in contrast, adopted the fork to avoid scalding themselves.

Lasagna was much appreciated as early as the thirteenth century by Salimbene de Adam, a Franciscan minor friar who traveled through France and much of Italy. Wherever he went, he knew how to appreciate the cuisine and to pinpoint what was best to eat. Lasagna, like all the pastas, was a relatively expensive food, really almost a luxury item, as documented by Sercambi. In story 58 of his *Novellas*, set in Venice, the daughter of Soranzo complains to her father that "her husband cannot afford to serve pasta as often as the father would like." That the lord in story 143 was a Spinola confirms pasta's luxury standing: "He took pleasure in eating pasta and sought comfort in farinaceous foods." The hero in story 60, ill for more than twenty days, was cured by "a regimen of capons, good lasagna, and other delicacies." Pasta was a restricted food, dreamed of by the less fortunate who imagined a never-never land where macaronis and ravioli dangle from a mountain of grated Parmesan cheese (Boccaccio, *Decameron*, day 8, story 3). A Florentine businessman living in Genoa, Saminiato de' Ricci, transcribed a recipe for preparing lasagna in his "commercial handbook," reporting "you've never tasted better."

When Sara Sacchetti transcribed the uses of the fork, they were still linked to pasta (*Three Hundred Novellas*, story 124): "Then came boiling hot macaroni. . . . Noddo began to eat the macaroni, wrapping in the meat underneath. . . . Giovanni still had the first mouthful on his fork [il primo boccone sulla forchetta]." The story is set in the middle of the fourteenth century. The gesture of twirling macaroni on a fork must have been familiar enough to her readers for Sacchetti simply to use the verb (*avviluppare*) to evoke the image.

Change is inevitable more or less everywhere, but above all in the already large, ever-growing cities (Naples, for example) produced by the phenomenon of urbanization. If in Paris bread took on a highly important role (let us remember that in the cities bread was purchased daily to be eaten fresh), Neapolitans had replaced (albeit gradually) their usual meat and cabbage (hot pot or stew) with dishes based on spaghetti. Macaroni, which throughout the sixteenth century was the typical dish of the Sicilians, only later became Neapolitan, and the "leaf eaters of Naples" were transformed, as I have already written, into "macaroni eaters" (*mangiamaccheroni*).

This change in culinary habits was neither spontaneous nor a matter of fashion. It was an adjustment to match available resources and, given the times, to accommodate the need to conserve and distribute them. It also took advantage of opportunities to increase production by using more perfected tools, for example, by employing hydraulic energy.

Thus the marketplace was offered a product that, while maintaining the fundamental characteristics of fresh homemade or artisanal pasta, had the advantage of a longer shelf life. These products facilitated distribution, costing less, much less, yet retaining the prestige of pasta, still considered a luxury. Puglia, Sicily, Campania, and Liguria dedicated

FIGURE 10

Cauldrons on the fire, engraving from Bartolomeo Scappi, *Opera dell'arte del cucinare* (Works from the art of cooking) (Venice, 1570).

themselves to pasta production either because of the bur-
geoning demand of a growing population (Naples) or for
reasons of external commerce (Liguria).

These modifications in eating habits are only some of the
many signs of the dietetic difficulties of the Early Modern
age. The increase in population, especially as concentrated
in the cities, was matched neither by a corresponding
increase in the production of provisions nor by progress in
the breeding of livestock. Above all, in the larger kingdoms
of Italy wealth was concentrated in the hands of the nobility
and the clergy, while for the less wealthy classes there
existed no means of saving or forms of investment that
would allow them to create estates. It took little more than a
single famine or epidemic to put thousands on the pavement.
The people lived in fear of hunger even when they had ready
access to the basics. The middle range of the lower classes
measured their wealth according to the quantity of stored
supplies they had at hand: a man from Sarzana (near La
Spezia) recalled that he had sacks of grain, lard, and barrels
of wine and this made him feel rich.

Something of this feast-or-famine mentality is with us
even today. Though we can shop daily for provisions on the
ground floor of our buildings, we load our cellars with wine
and our pantries with oil and other of God's gifts, not to
mention cramming our refrigerators and freezers. Thus we
are compelled to eat frozen foods even in the absence of dis-
asters and ensuing famine.

Pasta made of soft malleable grain or hard-grained wheat
bran is a product eaten almost exclusively in the Mediterranean and from a certain time on mostly on the Italian
peninsula itself, including the Po Valley and the hills of the
Piedmont. By pasta I also refer to the semolina of couscous
and the pasta pellets of *kuskussù* found in the Islamic
Mediterranean and in the Christian Tyrrhenian Sea. We
must also take into account the wheat pasta eaten in northern

China and in Japan, countries usually thought of as consumers of rice or pasta derived from rice.

Pasta, as we know, can be fresh or dried. Fresh pasta is, and was, prepared with soft grain and that preparation could be either homemade or artisanal. Dried pasta was almost immediately artisanal and was produced with a cutter and a press, the latter being activated by human, hydraulic, or animal energy.

It is a fact that, at least in the Mediterranean, the tradition of dried pasta became popular, especially in Italy. In *The Travel Journals of the Rev. R. Pococke*, there is a letter to his mother dated December 19, 1733: "In Italy along the road we find bad, sour young wine; sausages and a soup with vermicelli served everywhere covered with grated cheese and pepper, without which it would be very good." The reverend was English, and the English, as is well known, have never tried to understand new flavors. Concerning the "bad" and "sour" wine, I refer the reader to chapter 17 for my comments. As for unseasoned pasta, I wouldn't dare disagree with an English reverend. The tourist is always right: he's the customer!

Macaroni iron

I started discussing the uses of the fork to convince the reader that the area encompassing the spread of pasta was, despite a few exceptions, an enduring zone of civilization: a civilization, more precisely, of pasta and the fork.

The fork became compulsory only much later to comply with good manners. Its use first spread in the world of pasta, especially of fresh pasta, which, as I have noted, was considered a special treat. And so doctors, inclined as they are to forbid everything that tastes good, found at the end of the fifteenth century that one shouldn't overindulge in "lasagna, corzetti, tagliarini, tortellini, and the like." The quotation comes from a collection of medical recommendations preserved in the library of the University of Genoa under the title *Medicinalia quam plurima*. We won't follow the advice of this doctor, but it will help us understand that already in the Middle Ages this kind of pasta represented a treat, a sin of gluttony. So if pasta appears rarely in recipe books (people made it at home or bought it from the artisans who sold it), we know nevertheless that its consumption was high, that it was liked, and that it was expensive, which made it even more appreciated.

Another kind of pasta deserves a few lines of commentary here: Provençal *crosets*. These made the long journey from north to south when *kuskussù* was still limited to North Africa. This type of pasta was prepared in two shapes: big (*grossi*) and small (*piccoli*) crosets, disks of pasta measuring perhaps one centimeter in diameter and hollowed out by thumb pressure, like some of the cappelletti from the region of Parma. In contrast to the big ones, the small ones were marked with a lengthwise slash a little more than one centimeter in length on the oblong shape. Crosets were like potato or flour gnocchi, only smaller, thicker, and therefore easier to preserve. Having become products with great sales potential, both big and small crosets began to be made with a mold. The big crosets were round, and the carved mold decorated them with heraldic emblems, arabesques, flourishes, and often with the initials of the owner of the mold. The smaller crosets were made with a mold that gave them the shape of a tiny sole, like the numeral 8, so that they would look like the handmade variety.

With the loss of dialects, crosets came to be called "baby shoes" or saddled with other precious and usually silly names. These were an attempt to replace the "shocking" labeling of pasta shapes with suggestive names (*bigoli*, *pici*, etc.) that referred to the male organ.

As for *corzetti*, these would have the honor, because of their shape and longitudinal cut, of bestowing their name in Ligurian dialect to the female organ (especially that of baby girls). Known in Naples at the court of Charles II of Anjou (at the end of the thirteenth century), *corzetti* became common in Liguria where they are still served both in local restaurants and in families blessed with memory of traditions. It is well known that rural areas carry on traditions longer; especially in culinary matters, they maintain handcrafted molds and traditional methods that cities have largely abandoned in favor of mass-produced pasta shapes formed using specially designed up-to-date equipment. *Corzetti* are produced even today in the Ligurian outback (Gavi, Mornese, etc.). In Genoa they are called valley *corzetti* (referring to the valleys of Polcevera and Bisagno) to distinguish them from those made from industrial molds. *Corzetti della valle* are made by hand and correspond perfectly to medieval descriptions of that pasta.

Everyone knows the Angevins loved the Puglia region and that Anjou belonged to the county of Provence. It should come as no surprise therefore that we find that the old-style *corzetti* made by hand in Ligurian territory are identical to Provençal *crosets* and to *orecchiette* made by hand in the rural centers of Puglia (where they are also called *strascinati*). (Let us remember that in Puglia today there are still two or three regions where inhabitants still speak Provençal as it was spoken at the end of the thirteenth century.) In the Abruzzi, oblong corzetti are still available, made by hand and called *strascinati* here as well. In Sicily, the name *curzettu* is still very much alive. The locals chased out the French at the time of the Sicilian Vespers, but they held on to *crosets*.

Tomatoes had not yet arrived from America, and sauces

including pesto were used more to accompany meats than to flavor pasta. Pasta was seasoned with lots of cheese and sometimes a bit of pepper. To overcome dryness one added broth or meat gravy, a tradition confirmed by the Reverend Pococke, the eighteenth-century English traveler already quoted.

The food model can be defined as a characteristic common to various arenas of civilization: people who live in this or that domain will try to adapt new foodstuffs to patterns of consumption that fit their particular model. I shall show this in detail when I take up American products.

Now, however, we need to recall a grain that entered Europe thanks to the Arabs of Spain. In the fifteenth century rice reached Lombardy and the Piedmont there, where, as at Vercelli, the two provinces merge.

Rice is a grain with higher yields than wheat. Though for a long time expensive and in short supply, rice was an essential component in the preparation of the "white food," which spread throughout Europe including Great Britain. It was an ingredient in dishes still customary on the Iberian Peninsula (*paella*) or else as an accompaniment, thus preserving distant traditions learned from the Arabs.

The consumption of rice remained limited to the rich or to those inhabiting rice-producing regions. The Arabs of Spain and later the Spaniards used rice cooked white and linked to dishes of fish or meat, as was usual with couscous or *kuskussù*. When other Mediterraneans availed themselves of rice they put it into vegetable soup (again, as with *kuskussù*). In contrast, the peasants of Lombardy, following their traditions, made of it a kind of flavored *puls*, or porridge, they called *risotto*.

Rice made itself at home in Europe, in the Iberian region of Valencia where the Arabs had created a splendid system of canals as in Italy itself, in Lomellina and Vercelli. Even today these are the major European rice producers, although the Italian areas of production have been considerably extended since the early days. Rice paddies attract mosquitoes, which carry with them an increased risk of malaria, but the profit potential of rice was high, so rice went on to join the staple foods of Lombardy, soon becoming a regional signature dish.

Whether originating in Valencia or in Lombardy, rice had a moderate diffusion. Areas of cultivation were not extensive, with the result that Europe and even parts of Italy turned to Asian producers. Nevertheless, rice came to be one of the traditional foods, rich in calories but unfortunately poor in glutinates (protein obtained from grains).

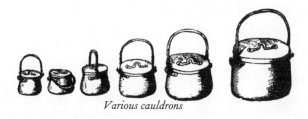

Various cauldrons

FIGURE 11
Engraving from Bartolomeo Scappi, *Opera dell'arte del cucinare*
(Works from the art of cooking) (Venice, 1570).

CHAPTER THREE

Stuffed Pasta

The tradition of stuffing pasta with meat, vegetables, and ricotta, or sometimes with both meat and vegetables combined, goes back at least to the thirteenth century. At that time Salimbene de Adam recounts having eaten ravioli without pasta (in Tuscany this is called *ravioli gnudi*, or naked ravioli), feigning to be shocked by this tasty variation. Clearly, in his era ravioli were already well known and had become culinary fixtures.

We are dealing here with pasta prepared under many different names: tortelli, tortellini, ravioli, *gobbi*, *pansotti*, *gattafure*, and so on, many of whose picturesque and sometimes metaphoric names, not to mention shapes, derive from the medieval cake, pasty, or *torte*. Sometimes they were called *pastelli* or *pasté*; at others, *altoscreas* (bread and meat), *empanadas*, and the like. The filling was almost always based on meat ground in a mortar and mixed with fats (lard) and various spices depending on the recipe. One could make *torte* with meat, fish (especially tench and eels), or crayfish from the rivers. For lean days or Lent, pasta was stuffed with ricotta and vegetables. Pasties were baked in an oven, whereas tortelli, ravioli, and the like could be boiled or fried.

The *torte* and *pastelli* were ancestral parents of our filled *pâtés* and *timballi* and of meat pies, give or take a few minor differences, of course. The meat, ground in a mortar, was reduced to a kind of mush. Then, flavored and spiced, the meat was placed on a sheet of dough set in a saucepan and then covered with another sheet.

A pasty could be made of ordinary bread dough or of a special dough much like phyllo or puff pastry, prepared with oil, fat, or rendered fat. Pasties were popular throughout the Early Modern era and have survived to this day with names, for example, like *pâté en croûte* or *empanada*. Under various other names pasties belong as well to the delicious cuisine of Sicily, where one can find fish *pâté en croûte*.

The statutes regulating bakers in Genoa during the thirteenth century refer to pasties filled with meat as *altoscreas* or *artoscreas*, the Greek term for bread and meat. Today the Greeks wrap meat or vegetables in layered dough or puff pastry (*pitta*) and label them variously *creatopitta* (filled with meat), *spanakopitta* (filled with spinach), and *lukanikopitta* (filled with sausage), the latter a kind of aristocratic hot dog.

The term *pitta* is still very much alive along with its variant (*pissa*) outside Greece in the area long known as Greater Greece and as far west as Marseilles, an ancient Phocaean colony. So *pitta* became pizza in Naples and *pissa* in Marseilles. The Turks early on adopted Greek cuisine and called these concoctions *dolmalar* (filled things). Since dental prostheses were not widely available and meat not always tender, the challenge was to make meat chewable and to season it as well as possible. Prepared in this manner, meat could be eaten even by the senior citizens (in those days anyone over fifty).

The filling of these dishes was dictated liturgically for lean days. For that reason, *torte* and *tortelli* filled with vegetables were not at all, as one might think, reserved specifically for the underclasses but rather symbols of veneration for the rules laid down for Fridays and for Lent.

For the peasant and especially for the kitchen gardener, vegetables were in the garden for the taking, along with the curd produced by the milk from one's own goat. In the big cities, however, despite the proximity of the kitchen gardens, vegetables, in relation to their nutritional yield, were more expensive than meat. The price of eggs, which could not be shipped in large quantities, varied according to the season. Flour for pasta was also relatively costly. So, surprisingly, what cost least was meat.

If ravioli, with or without meat, was a taste treat from the time of Salimbene, it was thus a treat more often available to those who were self-sufficient and produced their own food.

To devote an entire chapter to the topic of stuffed pasta might seem inappropriate. I think it essential nonetheless to stress this way of eating that allowed the weakest to survive despite frequent famines. Not just to survive but to flourish thanks to the shrewdness of the cook. Today, seasoned dry pasta, soup with meat, paella, and so forth are called unique, autonomous dishes. Dieticians today tell us that pasta dishes are complete meals. And so they were as well in the seventeenth century, when circumstances forced one to be satisfied with little more.

What I have discussed here relates to the Early Modern era, but by and large its culinary roots sank deep into the Middle Ages and even earlier. Success in the fight to nourish oneself often depended on the cook's skill at concocting pasta dishes (stuffed or covered) and was clearly an ongoing concern, especially to the lower classes.

Pasta "spur"

FIGURE 12

Saltworks, wood engraving from Georg Agricola,
Bermannus sive de re metallica (Basel, 1530).
(Milan National Historical Photo Collection).

CHAPTER FOUR

Water and Salt

Just a quick nod here to two indispensable life-sustaining ingredients.

For the civilization of ancient Rome the supply of water was an obsession and required major public investment (the remains of Roman aqueducts are present everywhere in Europe). The Middle Ages, on the other hand, were slow in supplying population centers with aqueducts. Fernand Braudel mentions the Roman aqueducts of Segovia as among the oldest. The Arabs in Sicily and in Spain devoted themselves to those public works, which furnished water both for the public baths in the cities and for irrigation of the rice fields.

The Genoese boasted numerous public bathhouses, and their aqueducts drew water from the rushing streams of the Apennines, which they then channeled into canals on top of the city walls. Water was distributed by "cannons," that is, through bronze pipes inserted at the corners of each gate in the city wall.

Though now preserved as cultural monuments, aqueducts constructed to irrigate the fields of sugarcane decorate the plain of Ficarazzi in Sicily even today. In Tenerife one can still admire the aqueducts built by the Genoese for the same purpose. Once again water had an importance that went well beyond the act of drinking. All the more so in fact because the rural world drank a byproduct of wine that as late as 1950 was called *vinetta*, *vinello*, *mescetta*, and the like. Widespread among the peasants, this drink was basically water containing the very last residues of the grape pressing; it was acidulous, watery, pink in color, and consumed in vast quantities to replace real wine, which was produced primarily to be sold.

In northern Italy each peasant was entitled to one or more strips or rows of vines planted along the perimeters of the fields. From the harvest of these rows the peasant could produce a certain amount of wine. A bottle, be it among the worst tasting, might be saved for festive occasions, but most of this wine went to the taverns that straddled the roads and were in the vicinity of river crossings. So the peasant was not a mere sharecropper but got some money for his labors. And, while this may be stating the obvious, this countryside *vinello*, with its vinegary taste, was certainly less infested with pathogenic germs and bacteria than straight water supposedly considered drinkable.

Salt was a product controlled by the government ever since antiquity. In the Middle Ages every feudal lord tried to collect a tax either on salt consumed within his fiefdom or on the salt in transit through his territory. J.-C. Hoquet and Pierre Laszlo have provided definitive studies of this topic. Here I need merely recall the nutritive importance of salt and its use in preserving foods, for example, what we now call *salumi* (delicatessen). It was not by chance that the Venetians launched their city with a splendid fortune earned from commercializing the salt from Chioggia that they carried from the mouth of the Po as far as Pavia.

Jug

Vieni di questo cascio háurai buon saggio,   Se uorrai regallar, condir uiuande,
Se uorrai saporir dolci beuande   Non ti dispiaccia il piacentin formaggio

FIGURE 13
Cheese seller, engraving from *Arte per via* (Bologna, 1660).

CHAPTER FIVE

Cheese

Marcel Mauss wrote that the Celts' was a civilization of cheese and cold cuts. One cannot fault him on this, but it is wise to take one additional piece of information into account: northern Europeans, in contrast to Mediterraneans, long maintained their capacity for digesting milk, thereby absorbing calcium despite the lack of vitamin D from the sun. They adapted their culinary practices to the climate of their country.

In his book *Good to Eat*, Marvin Harris devoted many convincing pages to lactose intolerance and its consequences. Here are a few complementary facts on dairy products both in Europe and in those countries Western Europeans call the Middle East, not to mention India.

It remains true in many cases that the inhabitants of hot and temperate regions do not tolerate milk well despite the recent "Bevete piú latte" (drink more milk) rehabilitation pushed in expensive advertising campaigns. It is also true that those who from early adolescence lose their capacity to digest milk do not stop needing and using calcium. Instead of absorbing calcium through dairy products, they do so thanks to sunlight. When ingesting milk became necessary—at what point in history is hard to pinpoint—milk transformed into yogurt, ricotta, and other cheeses became a food of necessity: predigested milk, as it were.

The geography of cheese and yogurt provides a story of great anthropological interest tied to the varied species of herds: cows, sheep, and goats but also to horses and in more recent times, among the bovines, to the water buffalo sub-species.

The production of cheeses in France and in the Piedmont offered the most extensive range and diversity according to the breed raised. I hardly need to mention that cheese from cow's milk allows the maximum production per unit and therefore per farm. Nor need I observe that cows produce more milk than any other competing species. But in Mediter-ranean countries sheep were in far greater supply. They were so numerous even in England that Thomas More wrote "sheep and men fed on each other." Production of cheese varied in Europe depending on the breeds raised, the kind of pasture, and of course marketplace demand.

A down-market product with a strong smell, goat cheese was certainly not appreciated at the tables of the Parisian aristocracy. Goats were bred to furnish skins for gloves and, above all, for goatskin wine pouches and water bags; cheese was thus a by-product. Quick to dry out and to change in taste and smell, goat cheese was meant to be consumed fresh. Distribution problems made it a regional product.

On the other hand, cheeses made of sheep's milk were eas-ier to conserve and to transport (they are mentioned in the Middle Ages, the Tuscan *ravigiuolo*, for example). Pecorino from Sardinia and Corsica was sold in large quantity in Genoa and shipped from that port city to the Ligurian out-back and other Mediterranean ports.

With the exception of some highly regarded products already famous in the seventeenth or eighteenth century (perhaps even earlier, though I have no first-hand documen-tation of this), fresh cheeses had to be eaten in their region of production. Here I shall give priority to products distributed to a broader marketplace, products that could withstand extensive shipping for retail in the cities. The market in fact is an urban phenomenon: the demand of the cities orients sales and consequently production. One need only consider the size and importance of cities like Naples, Paris, and London, as well as Genoa, Milan, and Venice, to understand this relationship.

A wholesale and redistribution center of produce such as Genoa in the sixteenth, seventeenth, and eighteenth centuries offers a privileged vantage point for these transactions. This port city was an emporium where products arrived from throughout the Mediterranean (in fact from the whole world) to be shipped both inland and to other port cities.

Canestrato and pepper cheese produced in Sicily as well as similar cheese products from Majorca were a great success throughout the Early Modern era thanks to the ease with which they were conserved and transported as well as their agreeable taste. Pecorino cheeses from Sardinia and Corsica sold well on the continent; because they could be transported by sea, shippers could take advantage of low freight costs. These cheeses, intended for popular consumption, took the place of the much more famous Parmigiano and Piacentino, which were more expensive and in addition had to be to be transported by mule across the Apennines. In any case, Parmigiano was present on the tables of the rich in Italy, France, and Spain and at times, although to a far lesser extent, was available to satisfy the demands of the poor.

Transportability also made the fortune of Dutch Edam, found in the knapsacks of French soldiers engaged in the war against Holland! The Dutch merchants obtained permission to cross the battle lines to bring their cheese to the enemy army. Edam invaded Europe and even reached America. It was on the tables of the Genoese in the first quarter of the eighteenth century, and at the end of that century, when the French presence created a crisis, it took the place of Piacentino in the pantry of the brothers of San Giacomo di Cornigliano. Its spread, however, began as early as the sixteenth century.

In Paris, at the table of the rulers, goat cheese was held in contempt, and the varieties consumed were few in number. The variety of products available was already great, however. Not all food was intended as luxury produce: taste sometimes knows how to resist fashion.

The country houses around the big cities produced vegetables, farmyard animals, and fresh cheeses intended for the urban markets, where greengrocers were allowed to sell cheeses in shops, thereby inciting complaints from the poulterers and cheese mongers. They sold rennet, ricottas, small cheeses of sheep or goat's milk, curds, and mascarpone. The market gardeners brought the freshest produce to town every morning, along with the greens from their patches.

Documentation is furnished by a contract in which a greengrocer paid a breeder a considerable advance for his output of curd. In Genoa, between the fifteenth and sixteenth centuries, there were around seventy cheese merchants, to which cohort one must add the itinerant pushcart sellers and Corsicans from Bonifaccio (authorized to sell their island products). Despite this plethora of sellers in a city of around seventy thousand inhabitants, there was room for illegals who, although often captured and fined, persisted, as evidenced by documents saying they were punished as recidivists.

si fa lauoreri di latte

nenene si fa

Luochi freschi doue fa lauoreri de latte

latte mele si fa

FIGURE 14

Milk production, engraving from Bartolomeo Scappi,
Opera dell'arte del cucinare (Works from the art of cooking)
(Venice, 1570).

I do not like summary restatements of the obvious, but the fact remains that cheese was widely distributed and consumed. The immense flocks in England and Estremadura in Spain and the great herds of all Europe that provided wool, meat, and skins also furnished milk and cheese.

During the entire history of the Early Modern period, the linkage wool-skins-milk-cheese-meat for sheep and goats and cheese-milk-butter-leather-meat for bovines had a notable effect on the prices of the by-products of breeding livestock, which could be accelerated or increased by strong and variable market demand. An increase in the demand for wool, for example, incites an increase in sheep flocks in order to make production meet demand. For expediency's sake, I will call this demand for one of several possible products *dominant demand*.

Cheese grater

To satisfy any dominant demand one needs to increase the size of the herd, which provokes a corresponding increase in the production of milk and cheese, skins (lambswool and fleece), and meat. If wool, for which there is strong demand, maintains its price, one cannot predict whether demand will increase for other sheep by-products. Thus one faces an increase in supply and perhaps a possible decline in the price of cheese and especially milk and meat. These products cannot be stored, and the demand for them may become rigidly stabilized even as the supply expands.

For the bovine herd, the primary product may be cheese (in Parma-Reggio-Lodi or Holland, for example), which is desirable for its high quality, its marketability, or its capacity to satisfy an international demand stronger than that for other products. In the three centuries of the Early Modern era, demand for cheese continued to increase, so the breeding of cows had to increase as well. Since cows provide milk after giving birth and since (chromosomes will have their say!) not all offspring are female, there had to be an increase in the total livestock headed for the slaughterhouse, which increased the supply of meat in the absence of a demand for it. The result was a stabilization of the price of meat and a noteworthy solidification of revenue, other sources of which were leather and butter, which I shall deal with later.

In passing, I must note that the tallow drawn from sheep fat could be used to make thousands of candles and that it was also used in significant quantities to grease spillways at the launching of ships. Tallow was so valuable that it was retrieved and recycled after each launching.

The food resource *cheese* was thus tied to the resource *meat*, which I shall treat in the next chapter, where I shall further show how dominant demand, by shifting from one to another product in the same grouping or category, can increase the supply of all the other products, which then become secondary compared to the object of dominant demand, be it private or public.

FIGURE 15

Butcher. Engraving from Diderot and D'Alembert, *Encyclopédie;
ou, Dictionnaire raisonné des sciences, des arts et des métiers* (The
Encyclopedia; or, Dictionary of sciences, arts, and trades)
(Paris, 1772).

IL
TRINCIANTE
D I
M. V I N C E N Z O
C E R V I O,
*Ampliato, e ridotto à perfettione dal Caualier Reale
Fuforito da Narni,*

TRINCIANTE DELL'ILLVSTRISSIMO,
& Reuerendiss. Sig. Cardinal Farnese.

CON PRIVILEGIO.

IN VENETIA, MDCXXII.
Appresso Alessandro de'Vecchi.

FIGURE 16

Frontispiece from Vincenzo Cervio, *Il trinciante*
(The carving-knife) (Venice, 1622).

CHAPTER SIX

Meat

Eastern Europe and much of central and western Europe offered vast spaces for breeding and raising livestock. During the Early Modern era demographic pressures were not yet intense enough to force the conversion of grazing lands into wheat fields or reduce the extent of pasturelands below the threshold of productivity. We must remember that a decrease in the area intended for pasture is not directly proportional to a reduction in the number of animals raised. If less than an appropriate given area is devoted to pasture, raising livestock commercially is no longer economically sustainable (except for domestic husbandry, which is hardly the same thing).

In Italy, where the plains were dotted with myriad towns from which issued a strong demand for grain, farmers drove their herds to graze on summer pastureland high in the mountains (transhumance). This alternative seasonal possibility of feeding flocks of sheep and herds of cows meant that meat, especially beef, was available nearby in all of Europe and as far east as the Ottoman Empire.

As for beef itself, we need to take into account the strong demand for leather driven by the Florentine market: with

leather one produced shoes, boots, saddles and harnesses for horses and mules, suits, belts, purses, and an endless array of objects that today would be made of plastic, rubber, and so forth. Halfway through the fifteenth century the Venetian Giacomo Badoer shipped thousands of preserved ox hides from Constantinople to Venice. In the middle of the seventeenth century Baccio Durazzo, originally from Genoa, bought and shipped thousands of skins from Smyrna. These two examples should suffice as illustration. All these beef cattle, whose skins were bought and sold, were neither buried nor burned; instead they provided meat to the entire Anatolian peninsula, either as fresh meat or as dried meat meant to supply the army. In this example the demand for leather was the dominant demand, as exemplified by the ample importation of leather from America and later by the settlement and creation of the huge ranches of Argentina. Export and import of meat itself had to await the launching of refrigerated ships.

Along the Danube as far as Pannonia and Germany there arose numerous livestock farms intended to feed central Europe. It was precisely there that a huge distribution center was created from which Venice and Genoa but especially Austria, Hungary, and Poland drew supplies. From Germany, pickled beef tongues came into Italy, where it seems they were much appreciated. Of course, Germany is the homeland of beef conserved in the form of cooked sausages (*Würstel*). At a time when false teeth were not yet available, ground, flavored meat had a practical as well as gastronomic appeal.

Raising livestock was also important in Italy. Differences in price allowed one to distinguish those areas where the product was superior (Moncalvo d'Asti, for example, was the market favored by the Genoese). It would seem that we are dealing here with a kind of biotechnology intended to develop quality meat products while also ensuring that the towns had a steady supply for the shoemakers as well.

In addition to importing cattle herds from the East, Germany, France, England, and Denmark autonomously produced excellent meats. And of course cattle breeding and raising livestock were important on the Iberian Peninsula and in the rest of Europe.

Cleavers

I mentioned leather at the beginning of this chapter to make the point that from a cow or an ox one derived more than meat and that this fact allowed the distribution or spread of costs and especially of revenue. At times leather might be more in demand than meat, so one slaughtered a cow more for its skin than for anything else. Cattle purchased at the breeding site were brought for slaughter to various towns. Except for the wages of the cowherds there were no other transportation costs: meat travels on its own legs. Livestock was therefore less expensive to market than other products that had to be transported via inaccessible roads on muleback.

Near the large cattle herds were found the peasants' modest livestock: two or three cows to give milk, produce calves, and help in tilling the fields. There were also calves raised with special care on private property, that is, by the owners of the land, in order to obtain the most desirable meat. In the Piedmont, one said that this home-raised veal was *à la façon du particulier* (today we would say "customized"). The veal calves were sold to the city butchers and then added to the yearly list of provisions inventoried by the authorities of the Annone. Often the butchers negotiated partnership contracts with the small farmer in order to have veal calves at their disposal even when the larger cattle markets were in difficulty. Nor was there a shortage of rural entrepreneurs who hoarded cows on the farms and estates near the town.

Butchers' knives

Oxen were used to work in the fields and to pull carts. When the last labors of fall had been completed (harrowing, for example), the aging animal was shut in its pen and fed on cereals, hay, and other grasses—in short, fattened for sale and ultimately for slaughter. At Christmas, it yielded a big boiled meat dish and the broth for cooking pasta, usually thick macaroni. This was not a tradition but rather a habit born from the desire to use the ox for fieldwork up to the very last.

Meat from the ox, the cow, and the steer was rather tough and chewy, if tastier. Veal was the preferred meat, a food, however, for the more prosperous classes, costing about twice the price of steer.

Jean-Louis Flandrin writes that until the end of the Middle Ages the French aristocracy scorned beef and preferred other meats, such as poultry and above all game. In the Early Modern era, however, consumption of butchered meat became valued once again. In the Mediterranean, veal maintained its rank and, along with beef, was purchased throughout the sixteenth, seventeenth, and eighteenth centuries. Veal was meant for the master's table, beef for the servants.

Servants enjoyed beef five days a week, and a pound of beef per person was served thrice weekly in hospitals. In Genoa a pound of beef cost two *soldi* in the sixteenth century and little more in succeeding centuries. In the same city the lowest salary, that of a boy helper or a cleaning woman, was

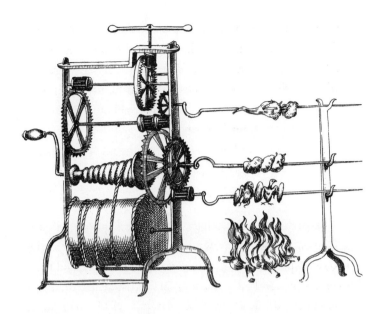

Molinello con tre spedi che si volta dasse per forza de notte con il tempo a foggia di orologio come nella presente figura si dimostra

FIGURE 17

Meats on a spit, engraving from Bartolomeo Scappi, *Opera dell'arte del cucinare* (Works from the art of cooking) (Venice, 1570).

six *soldi* a day, whereas an adult male could earn from ten to fifteen *soldi* daily, according to his occupation. A cook earned from two to four *lire* per day, and a cook's assistant or sous-chef one or two *lire* (a *lira* was worth twenty *soldi*). To sum up, with the minimum salary one could purchase three pounds of boneless beef, a quantity of protein sufficient for a whole week. Orazio Cancila confirms the same price range and general availability of butchered meat in Palermo.

Beef was therefore not a luxury product but one of the most accessible foods, consumed in quantities that today would seem excessive. Given that meat cost relatively little, butchers thought up pricing it on a sliding scale according to the cut; thus the custom arose of making fillets more expensive than haunches and saving the tripe for the less wealthy. Documents from eighteenth-century Paris confirm this. The ancient pride of the Germanic peoples had become a daily ration with little prestige, so the nobles had to turn their attention to game, fish, and other meats more expensive than beef.

England and Spain nourished within their respective confines countless sheep from which they derived wool, rams' skins, and parchment. The tails of Persian and Turkish sheep yielded a fat that replaced lard (forbidden by Islam). From the fat tails of English sheep there came a delicacy still appreciated today. Thomas More wrote that in the British Isles sheep devoured men, meaning that land was above all devoted to pasture. Whether in England or Spain, however, men certainly fed on mutton and lamb, not to mention the sheep themselves, which, when slaughtered, ended up cooked in various ways (boiled, for example). Flocks were so numerous it would not astonish me if the basic food of these countries were above all mutton, a meat both more tender and more flavorful than beef. Especially tasty was lamb, the prescribed meat for Hebrews as well as for Christians and Muslims in celebrating Easter or spring festivals. Since lamb was an ordinary food, the English lords preferred beef.

The guard of the Tower of London is called a Beefeater, and enormous roast beefs tower over their banquets.

In European cities lamb cost the same as other meats and sometimes a bit less. Shoulder of lamb was sold on the bone, and the yield in edible matter was therefore quite a bit less than that of a slice of beef. The same is true for the haunch, not to mention the rest of the cow. Lamb and goat were never alternative meats to beef if by alternative one means greater convenience. These meats were tenderer, tastier, and sometimes more expensive, especially in northern Italy and in France, at least in Paris, where urban crowds and cultivation had expropriated large areas of grazing land from big herds. Recall too that ever since the Middle Ages Italy was a big importer of lamb's wool and early on replaced parchment with paper.

The greater part of my documentation derives from the archives of cities where herds and flocks were brought for slaughter and meat distributed through a network of butchers and slaughter shops. There was a great variety of production sites where one could obtain a modest amount of meat at a low retail price or else butcher an injured or aged animal, using all its parts thanks to the shrewdness that thrifty kitchens always know how to manifest. The breeder had available the meat, which he preferred to sell, and the dairy products, which he willingly sold but from which he also fed himself, hoping to save the animals for sale and for breeding. Finally he sold the skin, which often was more profitable than the meat.

From goatskins he crafted gloves, leather for binding books, pouches (wineskins) to transport wine and oil, and so forth. The pouch was a skin turned inside out, with the skin on the inside stitched so that the contents would not leak. I hardly dare think what might be the taste and bouquet of oil and wine stored in such wineskins, but they were convenient containers for transportation, especially on muleback.

In the regions of greatest olive oil production—western

Liguria, for example—goats were raised to furnish skins. Since the pouches were produced by the hundreds, hundreds of goats were needed. The meat and milk (transformed into cheese) were secondary products offered for popular consumption. Goat meat was available in great quantities in the valleys of production and became inexpensive daily fare. Shoemakers and tanners, with the help of contracts drafted by notaries, appropriated all the skins a slaughterer might produce in a year. The butcher considered the skin and the horns the "fifth quarter" of the ox (this locution is found even today in the traditions and special jargon collected by chambers of commerce).

Skewer with wheel

I shall discuss pork later when I deal with sausage products, rich with added commercial value. Salami, pork belly, and hams are far more profitable than fresh meat, although in some European regions and later in America open-range breeding of hundreds of animals offered the possibility of adding fresh pork to the popular diet.

The raising of farm pigs involves labor costs, and feed had to be obtained by the breeder. Wild or semiwild pig farming costs less and offers a quality product with respect to the yield in meat. Germany and France, with their great forests, put large quantities of pork on the market at prices accessible to many. The Italian Apennine farmers raised pigs, as did to an even greater extent those in the southern Apennines, where one could purchase an entire herd of pigs to drive to the cities of the peninsula. Iberian pig farmers are still renowned for the products of their sierra.

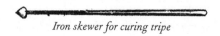

Iron skewer for curing tripe

To complete this review of meat resources available to the lower classes (and not always disdained by the ruling classes), I must note that horses, donkeys, and mules made a more than negligible contribution to the food chain and therefore to the production of leather and hides as well.

The cavalries of Charles V, François I, and Suleiman the Magnificent wore out thousands of saddles and harnesses (not to mention the leather used for the halyards of sailing ships and other leather products). The horses were slaughtered when wounded, and their meat was, and is, appealing and edible. Donkeys yielded very good meat, and mules, which by the thousands tracked along mountain trails, provided meat intended for sausage (blended with pork and pork fat).

Muslim enclaves, later absorbed into Christian society, left a legacy of consumption of salt-preserved donkey, horse, and mule. Mandrogne, in the Piedmont, kept up this custom at least until the 1950s. If this custom were ascribed to small Islamic enclaves, we would not be astonished, but I prefer to put forth an explanation confirmed for me by the fact that evidence for the consumption of horse, donkey, and mule flesh is found above all along the roads that lead from Genoa to Milan and from Genoa, via Cremona, to Venice, roads frequented by thousands of mules, donkeys, and horses.

As for meats produced by salt-curing horsemeat, these were not preserved to prevent spoilage nor to add commercial value (if there were any it would be slight) but rather to make edible a product that would otherwise be too tough to chew.

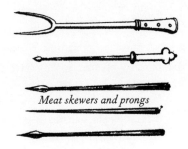

Meat skewers and prongs

FIGURE 18

The cooking of the meats, woodcut from Cristoforo Messisbugo,
Banchetti compositioni di vivande et apparecchio generale
(Banquets, foods, equipment, and utensils) (Ferrara, 1549).
(Rome Casanatense Library).

CHAPTER SEVEN

The Farmyard

Every barnyard, every farmhouse could raise chickens and rabbits, and with the latter the skins, if abundant, yielded greater profit than the meat. Roosters were destined for the market; hens, for the production of eggs. For the market in rabbit meat, one had to sell the rabbit at the beginning of the seventh month. During the first six months the animal grows at a rate more than just directly proportional to its maintenance costs. After six months, however, growth becomes less than proportional, resulting in production costs higher than possible profits. What applied to rabbits raised for meat, however, did not hold true for rabbits bred for fur and skin (with which one produced felt hats). These rabbits were raised for much longer than six months in order to obtain adult skins, stretched to the rabbit's maximum dimensions. The meat that was a by-product went for family or village consumption.

Hens produced eggs that peasants took to town to sell. Roosters, for the most part, were castrated and turned into capons. Chickens, pullets, and hens were transported live to the towns and resold by poulterers (a practice continued until a few decades ago). Poultry dealers kept the chickens and rabbits alive in the appropriate coops and warrens, butchering them at the time of sale. The absence of refrigeration did not allow for supplying slaughtered animals, and preparing them (shearing, gutting, skinning) was very labor intensive. Flocks were relatively sparse since there was no inexpensive feed available. It was better to keep hens for their eggs; the capons were ready by Christmas. Chickens and pullets were comparatively expensive and remained so until the spread of modern breeding methods and the availability of feed derived from fish by-products. Even urban families got the habit of keeping a hen in the house, perhaps on the top floor or in the kitchen in an open space under the sink.

Rabbit meat seems to have been reserved for popular consumption and as food in public taverns. In Italy the presence of rabbit was limited primarily to the domestic household economy. Elsewhere, as in Spain, production must have been much more important, judging by the numerous shipments of rabbit skins from Iberian ports. This animal was widely considered as wild game, especially in Spain and England, which attitude might explain the large numbers of rabbit skins exported from these countries.

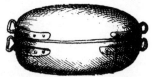

Food storage container

Goose had considerable prestige. On the plains of the Vendée, in Alsace, Hungary, Lombardy, and Friuli, great quantities of geese and ducks were raised to produce fat, flesh, goose liver, and down for stuffing quilts and pillows. The goose sausage produced in Lomellina was apparently mostly meant for the Hebrew community, for reasons anal-

ogous to those that fostered the consumption of horse meat in the Islamic community.

Again, despite my personal predilection for anthropological explanations, I must acknowledge that economics has its importance here: the dominant demand had evolved to goose down and foie gras. From the leftovers you could make sausages. Finally, ducks often seemed like game and were less common than geese (which were bred in quantity), or else they were widespread in a wild state that made them desirable and tastier. It remains indisputable that as food duck had considerable success among the well-to-do (one thinks of duckling or *caneton*) and that duck foie gras is now generally more appreciated than that of the goose.

Brass colander

FIGURE 20

Saltwater Fish (use of nets in fishing), engraving from Diderot
and D'Alembert, *Encyclopédie; ou, Dictionnaire raisonné des
sciences, des arts et des métiers* (The Encyclopedia; or, Dictionary
of sciences, arts, and trades) (Paris, 1772).

CHAPTER EIGHT

Fish

Mediterranean culture has mythologized the sea as a place of danger, of high-risk travel (need we recall Ulysses?), allowing for speedy and inexpensive communication and transportation but always perilous. Medieval freight bills and maritime registry documents as well as colorful regional locutions from the more recent past remind us that when the sailor finally ties up at dockside he has reached "salvation," a haven of safety.

Ulysses passed the pillars of Hercules and perished on the open water. The sea, it is said, does not like the curious. Only in the countries bordering the Atlantic and North Sea is it viewed as a resource, never in the Mediterranean and even less on the islands there. In the medieval world power and riches are bestowed and dependent on those who own land and livestock (*pecunia* is a Latin term meaning both livestock and money).

A man without money is the very picture of death (*homo sine pecunia imago mortis*). The fisherman, away from land, risks his life to catch his food. He does not own livestock. Unlike farmers or cattle breeders, he never knows with certainty what he will catch or capture. If the sea is stormy he does not venture out and therefore does not produce. A storm can last for days, and the sea can be impassable for weeks. That means no catch, which in turn means hunger.

No one wanted to be a fisherman. As F. Carletti noted, "Spaniards maintained that doing this was most vile" (see chapter 15). Al Bakri, an Arab geographer of the twelfth century, recounted that in Tunisia land belonged to the Arabs. The marginalized Christians thus became fishermen, the least of occupations, one so insignificant that Jesus entrusted his Church to Peter, a fisherman, the lowest on the social ladder.

Scraper

The nobles, the warriors, the strong ate massive quantities of meat. Feudal lords were carnivores. The wealthy owned land, flocks, and herds; the butcher was an artisan who often became rich. Meat was forbidden on fasting days, but fish was not. One might conclude therefore that fish is not as nourishing as meat. This is not true (at least in part), but if eating fish is allowed during Lent, on Fridays, and on fasting days, this means that eating fish is considered to be like fasting. Moreover, "popular" fish, those caught in nets in large quantity or schools (mackerel, anchovies, sardines, etc.), were not appreciated by the wealthy, who preferred big, white-fleshed fish (bream, sea bass, etc.). These fish are caught serendipitously, as it were, even if relatively frequently, depending on the season. As catch they cannot be counted in advance but must be sought out. Therefore they are by definition expensive.

The nobles and wealthy classes competed to assure themselves of large fish for Fridays and Saturdays. They were willing to pay ten and sometimes twenty times the price of the best meat. The fishermen who sold these fish sometimes offered them to the nobles in exchange for favors, keeping for themselves only those that were less showy and then only during shortages of marketable catches or when faced with fish that had become unsellable because they were torn when pulled through the stitching of a net.

Voltaire observed in his *Philosophical Dictionary* that if a pauper gnawed on a mutton bone on Friday, he would go straight to hell, whereas, still on Friday, those who buy and eat expensive sea bream find the gates of paradise open for them. (The number of people able to appreciate the irony of Voltaire's irreverent remark was and remains limited, very limited.) Halfway through the seventeenth century an edict against a taverner in Vado Ligure informs us that the wretch had served a dish of meat on Friday. It proved a futile defense strategy for him to assert that the client was a foreigner: he still had to close shop for more than a week. Today starving Kurds land in Italy and refuse to eat pork; three or four centuries ago, the European peoples were afflicted with similar prohibitions.

Prejudices are spread above all among the poorest of the poor who are often ignorant and therefore lacking in critical discernment. This keeps them clinging to their convictions. What little they know they have been taught; it little matters whether it be true or false. For them, it constitutes revealed knowledge, and to modify certainty is painful. It is hard to acknowledge that one's ancestors might have been wrong. Nor is it easy to understand, as Bertolt Brecht used to say, that nowhere is it stated that what has always been must forever be. In short, ideology and myth are more convincing than history.

The fish of the poor were signs of their poverty, and of

poverty one feels ashamed. Only the most destitute, those who had given up their dignity altogether, could sink so low, and the poor felt ashamed to buy fish. Before the Second World War anyone who bought *potassoli* (*gadus poutassou*, or whiting) was pitied, especially by other poor people. At the river mouth of Imperia there were people who preferred not to eat rather than to be seen buying fish. The prejudice concerning different species of so-called pauper's fish lasted until recent decades, when anchovies began to rise in price until they became more expensive than white-fleshed fish. Now the rich bourgeois adore them and cook anchovies in the worst manner possible, the way they think fishermen would cook them. The Greeks would call this the revenge of fate, or Nemesis.

Let us return to history. The thousands and thousands of miles of Mediterranean coastline provided quality fish to the well-to-do and soup fish to those who had to be satisfied with them. As I have noted, Lent and Friday mattered for everyone, even if not in the same way,

Small fish did not even get as far as the valleys that opened onto the sea. Anchovies, and especially sardines, transported for hours on muleback reached their destinations much the worse for wear and were not at all appetizing. In the hinterlands anchovies were only known salted.

The valleys had a very valuable resource, the eel. Eel was a most important resource since it could be transported live and on arrival kept alive in the ponds the Romans quite aptly called fish ponds or pools (*piscinae*). For this reason cookbooks are full of recipes for eel and for lamprey (which also could be transported live), as well as for carp and tench, which also populated the fish ponds of princes and monasteries as well as those of the bourgeois and the millers who ran the water mills.

The valleys whose rushing streams flowed into the sea only a few kilometers from the mountains had another resource, for the mouths of these rivers were full of sturgeon. Sturgeon was found as well in broad valleys such as those of the Arno, the Po, the Loire, the Rhone, the Seine, the Garonne, the Guadalquivir, the Rhine, and the Moselle, not to mention the Volga, the Don, the Dnieper, and the Danube.

It is not by chance that cookbooks dealt mostly with freshwater fish recipes or that lake fish such as pike had a literature better known than that of many saltwater fish. The availability of a product means that it will be better known and thus a focus of culinary preparation. Freshwater fish, including sturgeon for certain geographic areas (the Arno and Po), were predictably available, whereas saltwater fish were always occasional even when in season. The head cook of the lord of the manor as well as the cook at the tavern were both tied to the imposed program of Friday, Saturday, Advent, and Lent. No one, however, could predict the size of the catch of quality saltwater fish worthy of the lord, whereas, in contrast, one could count on the availability of freshwater fish.

Four-legged
warmer with lid

The example of prawns is typical. If the Adriatic or the Baltic offered the possibility of fishing for scampi (it is no accident that it is called *nephros norvegicus*), available equipment could not reach the habitat of shrimp, to say nothing of scampi living more than two hundred meters below the surface of the Tyrrhenian Sea. This type of deepwater fishing was only made possible much later by steel, nylon, and mechanical traction: the first Tyrrhenian scampi were discovered in 1925; the first red prawns were harvested in 1930. River shrimp were caught by hand in the rivers and streams; these were the shrimp represented in various *tacuina sanitatis* in the Middle Ages.

The fishing equipment available to coastal fishermen consisted of nets and fishing lines in configurations still in use today. Obviously, neither nylon nor steel existed then, so rope had to be made of plant fibers chosen from those that absorb the least water. But once wet even these were heavy. Ropes, hauled by hand, had to pull the entire net into the boat or onto land. Nets were handmade knot by knot out of cotton thread. This meant that the cost of a net was very high, often more expensive than the ship itself (even propelled by oars or sail rather than by today's expensive motors).

Fishermen were hired with contracts that allowed them to share in the proceeds of the sale of the catch. With one share going to the ship, one proportionally to the guild or network, and another to the owner, the remainder was divided among the fishermen according to the seniority of the crew. The equipment and technical know-how available to the fishermen, if quite refined (so much so that certain fundamental principles have survived unchanged into our own time), did not allow for fishing at excessive depths. What was possible in the Adriatic or Baltic was not possible in the much deeper Tyrrhenian Sea.

Many old-time fishing techniques may still be in use today, but the development of nylon allowed the manufacture of nets from three to ten kilometers in length. These boulters (called *palamiti* or *parangali*) were said to be much more efficient, made of steel-reinforced nylon of a diameter able to withstand any traction. When attempting to land the biggest, fastest, and strongest fish, one could also use special lines of stitched-in steel that were difficult to cut even with

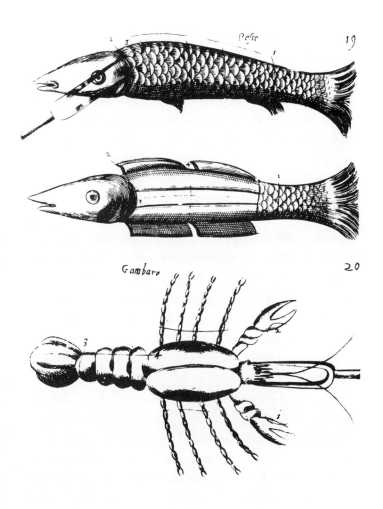

FIGURES 21 AND 22
How to Trim a Fish and a Lobster, engraving from Mattia Giegher, *Li tre trattati* (Three treatises) (Padua, 1639).

the best pliers. But back in the Early Modern era this equipment did not exist. One sailed *in paranza*, two ships trawling side by side, with the net dragged at a depth of only one hundred meters or a little more. This drew the attention of seventeenth-century legislators, who concerned themselves with outlawing trawling near the coasts and at certain times in the Tyrrhenian Sea. A seventeenth-century *parangale* (*palamito*) measured a maximum of around 250 to 300 meters. Today, as I have said, the length can attain several kilometers

I think all this makes it plain why fish products were so expensive. Folk (*gente* in the sense used along the coasts: seafarers) sought to fish as much in quantity as in quality but had no means of predicting their catch. Just a small drop in temperature at the water's surface could cause certain species to decline in number. Everything might well go to wrack and ruin when actual weather conditions belied meteorological forecasts in a particular season during which, under normal conditions, a species was apt to be available to fishermen.

Fish farming ensured a supply of tench, eel, carp, and sturgeon, which occupied a prominent place in the cuisine of the ancien régime. Lamprey, however, though much in demand, was not raised domestically and was protected by exclusive fishing rights as well as by minimal demographic pressures and the fact that mountain streams did not suffer from toxic pollution.

Eels could be stored alive in tanks for a long time. Tench and carp could be kept in the ponds of watermills or fisheries (from the fifteenth century on, in rice fields as well). The sturgeon that entered the fishponds of Mantua ended up on the banquet table of Prince Gonzaga of Mantua. Sturgeon could also be "milked," that is, one could extract their eggs (caviar). These were eaten without salting even by peasants, who used caviar to flavor their polenta, pouring it into the meal before cooking and then continuously stirring until the gray eggs were evenly distributed throughout the mixture.

Cookbooks also featured lake fish such as pike, tench, and carp, as well as other fish whose capture posed fewer dangers to fishermen than ocean fish because they had the good sense to inhabit rivers and inland lakes, where saltwater fish could not be delivered in good condition.

To reach a table in the heartland might take an ocean fish several days. To transport fish to Paris one might start at Le Havre and go up the Seine; for the Po Valley cities, one could travel upriver along the Po; for Rome, one arrived via the Tiber; and then there were the great rivers of the north. But how much time was needed? Too much for small fish, which would arrive rotten in summer and in bad condition whatever the season. Too much as well for fish heavier than one kilo. Transported to Florence from Leghorn (Livorno) on horseback at great expense they could hardly be moved more than about ten kilometers inland from the coast or mouths of rivers if they were to arrive in good condition.

To sum up, eating saltwater fish was very expensive even just a few kilometers from the coast. If you had to transport the fish over a mountain chain you might as well give up.

The distances that we measure in kilometers today were then measured in days. Even if at the right time of year someone might have succeeded in getting fresh fish to Rome or Paris, this would certainly have been a costly experiment, or else the fish would have had to be big enough to survive a lot of jostling. Anyone who has tasted fish on the Mediterranean coast and those of the distant hinterland knows the difference in flavor. But then the taste preferences of people living far from the sea are very diverse: the taste of fish in Moscow is intolerable to a coastal dweller, but Muscovites consider coastal fish insipid.

I hope I have made myself clear, and I do not wish to tire the reader with facts even more boring than those in the preceding lines, but to sum up: one links one's concept of the taste of fish to the particular flavor one is used to, and so cooks prepare dishes to taste the way a customer expects them to.

Since, with the exception of those that were hardy, like the eel, fish was difficult to transport, fish did not achieve the market distribution that its nutritional quality deserved. The result, in the Mediterranean and especially on the islands there, was the absence of a truly indigenous fish cuisine such as that developed, say, on the Iberian Peninsula, where fasting and lean days imposed by the mystic Philip II convinced the Spaniards to devise an extraordinary seafood cuisine.

Reasons altogether different led the inhabitants of lands bathed by the North Sea (the English, Dutch, Danish, Norwegians, and Icelanders) to create what has long been called "the civilization of the herring," which could also be called a culture of fish, and not only canned fish. The Atlantic and the North Sea offer a quantity and variety of marketable fish unequaled by the Mediterranean, where, aside from tuna, anchovy, sardines, and shad from the Nile delta, the catch was insignificant compared to the Atlantic (even the Portuguese and French Atlantic). Nor can one counter the statistical facts by reaffirming the nonetheless sacrosanct superior organic qualities of Mediterranean fish: gastronomy must not be confused with dietetics.

Pan for cooking fish

FIGURE 23
The death of the pig, eighteenth-century engraving.

CHAPTER NINE

Salt-cured Products and Sausages

Conserving foodstuffs has been a problem for a long time. The fear of hunger, the panic at not having provisions for the winter, and above all the awful spring (beautiful perhaps for painters and poets but truly terrifying for peasants and especially mountaineers) forced those living far from market centers to store food, not just meat but also fruit, greens, and vegetables. Examples of these latter are the many varieties of dried fruit, nuts (especially walnuts and chestnuts), chickpeas, string beans, broad beans, lentils, peas, and sauerkraut, either stored frozen under the snow or undercooked in vinegar or pickled in wine or apple vinegar as still occurs from Russia to Holland.

Food was stored for those months during which neither fresh fruits nor meat was available. It is still easy to point to those geographic areas where methods of conservation were possible on-site and were therefore more than elsewhere linked to climate and natural resources. (In countries dominated by mercantile economies freed in part from meteorological considerations and wholly from the availability of natural resources, these methods underwent a diversified development.) Norwegians north of Bergen exploited a climate suited for drying cod (stockfish), whereas the English and Dutch had to resort to salting (*bacalao*), like the Icelanders and Mediterraneans, who were favored with ready supplies of salt. If air-drying was not in order one could always turn to the smokehouse, which among other advantages allowed greater economy in salt usage (Austria, Bohemia, the Tyrol, etc., for pork; Ireland, Scotland, Norway, and Russia for salmon and sturgeon). These products, perhaps born from the need to face the unproductive months, quickly became familiar, pleasant dishes, much appreciated and eminently exportable.

The English and the Dutch fished for herring by the ton and even went to war over the monopoly on herring. We owe the Dutch a discovery of great importance: salting herring at the moment of catch. This happened around the middle or end of the fifteenth century, and from that moment on fishermen no longer needed to return to their home ports in order to salt their catch, which would have degraded considerably during the trip home. Now the herring lay salted in the hold of the fishing boat. Thus was obtained a far better product, because herring is rich in fat, and fats deteriorate quickly, to the detriment of taste.

Many years ago I called the world of the North Sea the "civilization of herring." I believe this definition is appropriate because herring had a vital function in the diets of the English and Dutch. The latter justifiably considered *maatje* a special treat (these are young herring eaten raw).

Salted or smoked, herring spread through all of Europe and brought protein at low prices to the population of the agricultural heartland, nourishing the body while sheltering the soul from the temptation of eating meat at forbidden times. (I suspect that the landlocked German population welcomed the Reformation as much as a liberation from their compulsory herring as a theological event.)

Protein was scarce, especially for the less fortunate and

especially for those living far from the big cities. There, supplies, however minimal, were guaranteed in order to avoid serious social unrest. On Fridays and Saturdays (and for all other fast days, as well as for the forty days of Lent in spring), meat and other fats were forbidden. Fish, however, was permitted and from it was derived a source of adequate protein.

On December 18, 1497 (five years after the discovery of America), Raimondo de Raimondi sent a letter from London to Milan addressed to Ludovico Il Moro in which he says of John Cabot: "His English crew said that they had so many fish that this kingdom will no longer need Iceland which produced a huge supply of fish called stockfish." As everyone will have surmised, this is a reference to the discovery of the Newfoundland banks, a discovery far more important than any so-called El Dorado.

Galicians, Portuguese, Frenchmen from Saint-Malo and Olonne, men of Biscayne, and then Dutchmen and Englishmen devoted themselves to intensive exploitation of the banks, spreading the consumption of cod throughout Europe, not only in maritime countries but also and above all in the agricultural heartlands such as central France and the Po valley. The fish caught on the Newfoundland banks is similar to Norwegian stockfish. It was marketed salted with the name *cabeliau* or *cabillou*; it was called *bacalao* (cod) on the Atlantic coastline of the Iberian Peninsula and termed *morue de Terreneuve* (Newfoundland cod) in a French recipe collection dating from the middle of the seventeenth century (Jean-Louis Flandrin, *Le cuisinier françois*).

Above all it was a salted fish. Dried stockfish remained a Norwegian product. Even when a way was found to dry fish from the Newfoundland banks, Norwegian fish kept its superlative reputation. Even today the bounty of Newfoundland thus dried is called *baccalà* or cod, but Norwegian catch is typically called stockfish. As for Italy, stockfish was

FIGURE 24

Saltwater Fish (salting sardines), engraving from Diderot and D'Alembert, *Encyclopédie; ou, Dictionnaire raisonné des sciences, des arts et des métiers* (The Encyclopedia; or, Dictionary of sciences, arts, and trades) (Paris, 1772).

distributed there mostly through charitable feeding stations (paupers' asylums, Catholic charities, franchised purveyors of hot meals for the poor, etc.). Toward the end of the sixteenth century, on lean days stockfish substituted for expensive fresh fish.

The port cities of the Tyrrhenian Sea preferred the Norwegian catch, marketed mostly by the Dutch but also in the eighteenth century by the Norwegians themselves. Distribution in the hinterland consisted mostly of Newfoundland fish. Arriving from far away, dried and salted fish quickly became incorporated into local dishes. One found cod everywhere, from Portugal to Provence, Barcelona, Genoa, Leghorn, Naples, Messina, and Palermo and as far afield as the banks of the Po and Adige rivers, Rome, and of course northward to London, Amsterdam, and the German cities that were the first (in the fourteenth century) to market Norwegian fish. Fish from Newfoundland reached Genoa from Marseilles at the end of the sixteenth century. From there it was shipped to the Piedmont and Lombardy heartland and toward the regions around Venice.

All this commercial success was doubtless due to the serious lack of proteins in the diet of the rural population, but in the market cities there was a different appeal. Among the *salumi* (deli fish), as salted fish was called, flattened fish sticks had come to replace back fish, that is, the dried and smoked sturgeon that hung in beautiful rows in cheese shops. After all, the price was more reasonable than that of sturgeon, which henceforth no longer made it beyond the Dardanelles. Italian sturgeon could no longer satisfy the demand. From a cultural point of view, this change was not traumatic. And the purveying of fish at charitable feeding stations had at least taught Italians that fish could be steamed or boiled just like meat. Fish *in scabeccio*—in brine—came to Genoa from Sardinia and Sicily to be reexpedited toward the heartland. Also shipped inland were boiled fish or fish overcooked in a boiling broth of myrtle rich in tannin. The myrtle gave the boiled fish a consistency sufficient to allow it to weather the long (six- or seven-day) journey. The applied recipe was recorded in Sardinia and in Genoese documents as "myrtle fish." In Italy, stockfish and cod came to be cooked in a variety of ways, without however reaching the almost one hundred recipes boasted of by the Portuguese. The preparation of fresh fish is, in contrast, far removed from what is normally defined as "cuisine" in the great majority of cases.

Since antiquity every conceivable kind of fish has been salted, dried, and smoked: sturgeon, eel, and other freshwater fish; tuna, mackerel, skate, sardines, and anchovies among the saltwater fish. I have already named the species that were marketable and therefore mentioned in sixteenth- and seventeenth-century fiscal and legal documents preserved in various Mediterranean archives.

In this ancient historical sea, tuna was caught with the appropriate tuna-fishing gear. After the conquest of Seville by the Castillians, it became an important source of income for the Medina-Sidonia family, which employed Arab workers (from whom came terms such as *rais* for boss and *musciammà* for dried tuna meat, among others). The Portuguese fished for tuna with lines and buckle tongues (hooks), unbaited so as to lose no time unhooking the catch. The Genoese very quickly developed tuna fisheries in Liguria, Sardinia, and Corsica and from the seventeenth century on guaranteed for themselves the monopoly of tuna in the Egadian islands. "Tuna is money," it has been said. The Genoese created a veritable hegemony in both the production and the marketing of tuna. This has also been confirmed for Sicily. For the Genoese tuna trade, there is the ongoing research by Nicola Calleri, who has given me his files on tuna in oil. He dates its spread to as early as the first half of the seventeenth century. If the practice of preserving tuna in oil was already documented in financial records at that time, it likely began some decades earlier. Tuna was also salted and shipped in barrels. The best cuts were meant for wealthier clientele; the lesser cuts were meant for mass consumption. But what is popular in one locale is not so everywhere.

The high cost of transport by land and the ecclesiastic need to feed on fish forced consumers to eat bait fish, which

Oyster-shucking knives

originated in Sicily and was called the "people's tuna." Compared to fish in brine and to bait fish, which was a poor substitute for herring, even the worst tuna seemed good: at least it was somewhat tastier and had a more appetizing color. And so tuna entered northern Italian cuisine as a delicacy, so much so that a clear-hued and tender meat properly cooked was labeled "tunalike." Various sauces were made with tuna, and other dishes in which there was only the slightest hint of tuna were nevertheless given forged letters of nobility.

Salt-cured anchovies, prepared on the beaches where they had been caught, were sent after a few months of seasoning toward the mountain passes and consigned to distributors, who sold them at fairs. So anchovies, with olive oil, were food for lean days during autumn, when the clumps of thistles in the Piedmont were ready for harvesting. For these meals the folk of Langa and Monferrato invented the *bagna cauda*.

The use of oil to preserve tuna came to extend to other fish: sardines kept better in oil, but much time would pass before they became a common food. The sealed tin can only came about with the industrial revolution.

Using oil in this way was (very probably) an idea born in Liguria, where it was usual as early as the sixteenth century to preserve porcini mushrooms (*Boletus edulis*) in oil. (They were also dried, these being the "Genoese mushrooms" mentioned in recipe collections.) Truffles were shipped in oil to Germany (*tuber magnatum*, or white truffle, and *tuber melanosporum*, or black truffle), where they are called *terra-trufe* in a seventeenth-century document, which refers to the tuber as *Toffeln*.

Not to be overlooked among the salted fish products available in the markets of the big cities was caviar. A luxury product today, during the Middle Ages it was shipped from the Black Sea to Italy. There, however, sturgeon eggs were harvested both on the banks of the Po and elsewhere, so while caviar may even then have been an exotic and expensive delicacy, the caviar eaten by the painter Pontormo certainly was not Beluga. Indeed, when it was "Italian caviar," or sturgeon eggs, it was fairly inexpensive. Often *bottarga* (tuna roe), which, like the Greek *taramà*, is simply produced from fish eggs, was passed off as the real stuff.

When the closing of the Dardanelles caused a shortage of caviar, the Italians—whose consumption thereof in the seventeenth century was the most lavish in the world (they didn't know about decadence but learned about it later, from the historians)—received deliveries of Volga River caviar from Dutch boats that had gone to fetch it from Murmansk. The caviar barrels also served an extra function, providing necessary ballast since the rest of the cargo consisted of skins and other goods that, though pricey, did not weigh enough to stabilize the ships. This double function also cut the shipping costs.

International events in recent times have had a negative impact on the price of caviar and made it a symbol of opulence. But in the Early Modern era, at least in the mercantile urban world, salted fish products retained for the longest

FIGURE 25

January: the kitchen, engraving by Antonio Tempesta from
I dodici mesi (The twelve months) (Rome, 1599).

time their reputation as food of last resort or Lenten food that one was constrained to eat either because none other was available or because meat was forbidden. For the poor, then, caviar was just another type of salted fish, and despite the price, the publicity, the prestige, and the exclusivity of the product, thinking people of modest means asked themselves whether it was worth breaking the bank for a "canned food."

In Milan, a few decades ago, one said of those who lacked means that they were "reduced to bread and little fishes," which corresponds to the English fish and chips. But though this was poor people's food, the salted, dried, and smoked fish that constituted a dietary resource for the people were also a source of wealth for entrepreneurial tradesmen and for small-time purveyors such as those who fried fish on the beach, put them in barrels with vinegar and oil (*escabece*), and transported them by mule inland.

Meats—beef and especially pork—demonstrate the trend toward conservation, though I must point out that the label "preserved meat" was dropped very quickly, except where (as on the Iberian Peninsula or in Anatolia) applied to dried beef intended mostly for troops on the battlefield. As for pork, sausages and air-cured hams became the dominant products almost immediately.

One must go back in time to understand how certain products having been local (*du terroir*) then became regional. Certain areas, like Piedmont and Lombardy, were deforested during the High Middle Ages, forcing the peasants and breeders to stable their pigs. Elsewhere, as in the Apennines, Friuli, the Iberian Sierras, and the forests of France and Germany, pigs continued to be allowed to graze in the woods. Animals raised in stables yielded lots of fat, though the meat of their thighs did not produce prosciutto hams since the muscles were not developed (the domesticated pig remains stationary for most of its life). These stabled pigs yielded cooked or raw salamis into which were poured the best parts, belly, lard, and so forth. The forested zones where the pigs ran wild through the woods and developed their muscles gave the best hams, to the detriment of salami production.

Casings filled with meat preserved in salt derived their name from the adjective, henceforth a substantive, and are

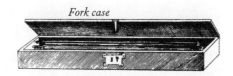

Fork case

called *salumi* (charcuterie, or cold cuts). We are dealing with meat here, and so with a customer-appreciated product much in demand. The epithet "Lenten food" and the status as replacement food for lean times inflicted on salted fish did not apply to salt-cured meat, except perhaps for beef pancakes and the *pastermé* of the Turks, the first intended primarily for sailors, the second for the troops (two unappreciated products therefore). Anyone who spent a year in the trenches during the 1914–1918 war or lived through the most recent world war, whether at the front or at home, would long shun any canned product—"soldier's food"—like the dried meat of the seventeenth century. Today, however, *pastermé* is served in Turkish restaurants under the name *pastirma* as a typical traditional dish, which gives it respectability. Basically it is dried beef, spiced and fried or else served cold, thinly sliced, as it is served in the Swiss mountains, where it is called *Bündnerfleisch*.

The conservation of meat takes advantage of the same methods described for fish: drying, salting, and smoking.

During the Early Modern era, Bohemia, Austria, and Hungary were destination points for the shipment of cattle from the Danube valley and also distribution points for eastern Germanic countries and for Italy, where German and especially Hungarian production was eaten when shortages or epidemics blocked supplies of local meats. It is interesting that in the Germanic countries, including Alsace, the Grisons, and neighboring valleys, sausage was made with both pork and beef (*würstel*, *bressaola*, etc.). The surplus—that is, that part of the livestock product not absorbed by industry—could be allocated to local or family consumption and to that end poured into casings and conserved. So a way of doing things arose that we inaccurately call "regional tradition" or "*terroir*."

The zones devoted to cattle raising produced dried beef or encased beef sausage, those devoted to porcines yielded cold cuts and hams. In Islamic countries, the sausage was made of lamb. And, as I noted earlier, meat did not carry the stigma of being a stopgap or replacement product, so beef sausage and especially salami and ham (in their various forms) were prized foodstuffs.

The transformation of pork into bacon, salami, cervelat, ham loaf, *mondiole*, cooked chops, trotters, and sausages was a godsend for the farmers. In Germanic countries especially, pork was eaten fresh. Where there existed a marketing system that could satisfy urban demand, the breeder could derive profits especially from the value added by processing his meats. I am not referring here to salted meats fattened for winter but rather to products rich in added value, destined for the marketplace. This does not mean that the peasant did not raise pigs for himself and for his winter protein supply or that all farmers had a strong market orientation: even today, in the Cantabrian mountains and some sections of Provence, diced salted pork is stored in the pantry and called *petit salé*.

But the *petit salé* of the Provençaux, the *cansalada* of the Catalans, and the salt meat of the Ligurians were rolled porkbellies produced for the marketplace or for the master's table.

Feeding a stabled pig entails costs that in turn affect the price of butchered pork. A producer risked not only just covering his costs but also incurring a loss when the market price fell. Therefore there was no advantage to eating pork fresh, except at times of great surplus, as happened in Germany. The breeder could, however, significantly enhance the value of the meat produced in butchering by preparing sausages and blood puddings, sold fresh to satisfy immediate financial expectations, and by producing bacon, pork belly, cooked and raw salami, hams, pork roll, calves' head—in jar or galantine—and *mondiole*, this last from Cremona and Piacenza and available in what was then the richest city in the world: Genoa. Each of these products needs seasoning or maturation ranging from a few days to several months and as long as fourteen months for the best prosciutto hams. Each prepared product can be sold at a price far higher than that of fresh pork. This is why, wherever the marketplace was lively and demand heavy because of dense population and purchasing power, it was preferable to transform a slaughtered pig into multiple value-enhanced products rather than to market it as fresh meat.

Of course, fresh pork was part of the popular diet, but that depended on the market, that is, urban demand. Possible surpluses, not unusual in parts of Germany, Spain, and France, where the cities were not as heavily populated as in Italy, were eaten fresh since the animal proliferated and one could get all kinds of food from it: suckling pig in Sardinia, milk-fed pork in Spain, pork roll in Umbria, all prepared with flair. The name "*norcino*" or "Norker" designated those who prepared and sold pork. In Genoa those who worked in pigskin and fine pigs' hair brushes were equally skilled.

For Grimod de la Reynière, the pig was an "encyclopedic animal," and this is so in fact, given the huge range of uses to which a pig can be put. I recall nonetheless what the great August Escoffier wrote: "Without the gastronomic value of its prosciutto hams, the pig would never have the place of honor it occupies in haute cuisine dishes." This relates to both the enhancement of the product and its added usefulness. Whatever has a place in the kitchen of Escoffier is worthy of a great table.

Charcuterie, or salt-treated meats, quickly became a delicacy for urban Europeans and a commercial resource for breeders. Already in the Early Modern era Modena was well on the way to becoming the capital of prosciutto, along with Parma and then the Friuli. Piedmont remained loyal to its own regional salamis, as did other regions, especially when they could count on market demand from big cities like Naples, consumer of products from Calabria, Campania, and the Abruzzi such as head cheese and *capicolli* pork sausage. Similarly, in Seville and other large cities in Spain the demand for Serrano ham induced the breeders to improve and enhance their product line with "blackfoot" ham (and done today to increase production). The region around Paris also produced hams, as well as foodstuffs less popular but nonetheless sought after as local specialties by urban populations of varying origins. Today Paris enjoys a confluence of produce from the French provinces. The city was a center of culinary exchange even in the Early Modern era, especially when the kingdom of France became a centralized state, summoning to the capital city people from all regions and all classes, all of whom were convinced that the foods as well as the wines of their regions were superior.

No one should be astonished therefore if the big cities of

the Early Modern era, though swollen by a large permanent population and transients that often pushed them to the brink of starvation, with their strong economic demand contributed to the transformation of our ways of eating and the spread of new food traditions.

Vi, giun afe da uenditore agrerte,
Ch io uiuo lasciar questo mestiere infame,

Poiche deggio qual Asino da certe
Altrui dar cibo, et io morir di fame.

2

FIGURE 26
Fruit seller, engraving from *Arte per via* (Bologna, 1660).

CHAPTER TEN

Vegetables and Fruits

Mediterranean consumption of fruits and vegetables was (for arbitrary and profoundly mistaken reasons) often linked to poor folks' cuisine, to peasants' or farmworkers' food. One can make teasing reference to Giulio Cesare Croce and his *Bertoldo* (quoted by Massimo Montanari in his *Convivio*), to medieval short stories, to the satire of the peasant (Merlini), and to so many other examples, using them to attribute culinary traditions based on agricultural production to farmers and peasants, that is, to the poor. This approach to understanding the quality of life is urban and above all courtly. The behavior of the farmer, his language, and his peasant ways are contrasted to the urban and the urbane whenever convenient.

The satire of the rustic, and its opposite, the glorification of his rural life, comes into literature according to the political whim of the moment: from the *Bucolics*, composed when the "holy" farmer (Virgil's *agricola*) resided in the countryside, to the satire of the bumpkin Matazone by Calignano and so many others, written when it seemed expedient for the people to go and swell the ranks of urban workers. From these extends a line that culminates in Arcadia, which exalted sheep raising and the pastoral life, contrasting them to the trying and tedious contradictions of the intellectuals of this century.

This is not to say that the peasant and even less the small-time farmer were always poor. Nor was it the case that their food resources were worse than those of city dwellers, artisans who bought at the market, or the man of letters who ate at the home of his patron. The products of the fields and the farmyard were available to the family farmer who grew them for the marketplace. The peasant had rights to his agricultural produce (exempt from feudal taxation) and to some of his livestock, with the exception, often, of the pig. This meant that for the small farmer green vegetables could be daily fare and could replace other foods; they were paid for by his labor and time but without real monetary expenditure. Thus, insofar as greens were produced by farmers who were often poor (being laborers, not soldiers or men of the word) and that peasants and dirt farmers ate the greens they did not sell (as was the case for fish with fishermen), one could describe this food as poor people's food.

This reasoning may seem sound, but seasoning scholarship with a bit of market reality reveals that, since they yield very little, especially when cooked, greens are expensive, and so in relative terms more expensive than meat. Obviously this isn't so in absolute terms, but the fact remains that 2 *soldi* purchased 300 grams of meat, while one artichoke cost 2.6 in December, three cardoons 8 each, a bunch of chicory root 4, and cabbage tops for soup more than 1 *soldo* apiece (in other words, two cabbage tops cost as much as three hundred grams of meat). Fresh greens, at least in the cities, were hardly poor people's food. Consider too that the price of eggs, variable by season, ranged from 5 *soldi* a dozen in June to 12 *soldi* in December. Compare these to the price of an artichoke!

These were the prices in Genoa at the end of the sixteenth

century, and those in other Mediterranean cities were more or less analogous. The situation in northern Europe and Paris was somewhat different. In Paris, in the Early Modern period, the consumption of expensive vegetables increased, according to Jean-Louis Flandrin, who wrote on asparagus, artichokes, and mushrooms. These latter are not really kitchen garden vegetables, nor even products of hothouse growing, which started early in Alfort, but rather meadowland products, what we now call champignons, which are very different from forest mushrooms. All these were imported, unusual, and expensive foods (and who knows in what condition they arrived on-site), meant to be eaten by the nobility of Paris. They were luxury items, suitable for conspicuous consumption and therefore indispensable on the aristocratic table.

Other greens still remained Mediterranean food. There, people, though convinced they must imitate the powerful and the pacesetters, did not give up their regimens of vegetables and pasta. The use and abuse of the tomato at the end of the nineteenth century have been demonstrated. Nor did the Spaniards give up vegetables. Thanks to tradition and cultural borrowings from many diverse peoples, they created a fine and healthy cuisine combining fish and vegetables (aided by the fact that Spaniards had to follow the directives of Catholicism anyway). Theirs was a great cuisine unequaled anywhere, unless one went as far afield as China, Japan, and Southeast Asia, where the Chinese aesthetic instructed that, cooked properly, anything edible could be good and healthy—as long as one excluded milk and its derivatives. Lactose intolerance defeated even Chinese pragmatism: milk caused immediate stomach pains, so it was eliminated. Consider too the example of Greece, where not the language but certain food habits (pastries filled with greens and stuffed vegetables) survived (and were adapted by) the otherwise overwhelming Turkish hegemony.

I have stated several times that "cuisine" is an urban phenomenon, one that has maximum potential for expression in the cities. This is true as well for the immediately surrounding countryside, the villas and the estates. There, the farmer used his produce for stuffed pasta and could mix the freshest clotted cream with herbs to fill his Lenten pies and those Pascal loaves stuffed with the eggs that the hens at the end of March—that is, at Eastertide—had decided to deposit in quantities sufficient to be brought to market or reserved for domestic consumption. (I prefer this expression to the term *autoconsumption* because, except for the candle, nothing tends to consume itself).

City dwellers, unlike farmers, had to buy produce in the markets. Artichokes, cabbages, radishes, and endives did not get to the city on foot like livestock. Vegetables had to be transported in carts and on muleback every morning. Farmers left before dawn to arrive in time to distribute their produce to retailers or to display it on stands or carts in their assigned and prepaid slots on the public square designated for the market.

The truck farmer does not live like the peasant of the fields: he changes crop plantings with the stages of the moon and lives in daily contact with the city and with money, which makes him very different indeed from the grain farmer of the prairie. The work of the truck farmer is certainly more demanding: the variety of crops and the care they require make him a skilled laborer, and as such he must be paid. The price of greengroceries is far higher than that, for example, of wheat. All this is reasonable enough, but the effect is to make those vegetables intended for urban consumption expensive.

City dwellers were used to this state of affairs and left the freshest early-growth crops to the well-to-do while contenting themselves with in-season produce, whose prices fell at the time of maximum production and availability. As for the less fortunate, they showed up at the market just before closing, at the moment of the sell-off. The produce purchased then was of lesser quality, but the price was more affordable. One entrepreneur began his career buying the leftovers of the Nice Monferrato market in the evening and reselling them to the poor. With this inspiration to salvage tired greens, he founded an empire.

To hold on to their valuable greens longer, the Germanic peoples invented (I don't know when) the conservation of cabbage by means of fermentation. The Alsatians and Swiss-Germans called it *Sauerkraut*, the French *choucroute*, the Italians *crauti* or *San-crò*, an inadvertent takeoff on sauerkraut. In the Germanic countries these acidulated cabbages serve as a bed for a sumptuous display of pork meats superbly cooked. From the Mediterranean islands came capers, both salted and brined in vinegar, which spurred a vibrant business. From the eastern Mediterranean, perhaps because of the Hebrew diaspora, gherkin pickles or cucumbers reached Sephardic Spain and spread from Greece through Russia and Poland (in apple vinegar) and from the Baltic down as far as Holland. Mediterranean capers, truffles, figs, lemons, and olives came to Germany via Amsterdam and from there (or from Venice) reached Poland.

A decree from the city government of Alessandria in the middle of the fifteenth century ordered all farmers to cultivate fruit trees—apples, apricots, plums, and peaches—whose fruit would be reserved for the landowners. In every vineyard some peach trees had to be grown. But as too often happens with standards written by legislators and not tested by experience, the law, which stated only that farmers had "to plant," did not have the intended effect. A lot of delightful peachtree saplings appeared in the vineyards that the peasants took great care to graft and cultivate. Pears and apples were likewise planted. But since no imposed norms

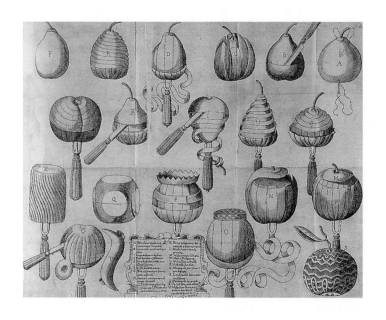

FIGURE 27

How to cut and slice fruit, engraving from Antonio Latini, *Lo scalco alla moderna, overo l'arte di ben disporre i conviti* (The modern steward; or, The true art of taking care of guests) (Naples, 1694). (Rome, Collection of the Casanatense Library).

spelled out what care was due these young trees, the peasants simply planted and forgot them, letting them grow willy-nilly.

Any fruit harvested was the landowner's property, controlled by and subject to their insistent demand. Fruit belonged to the table, to the "mouth" (an orifice limited to the landowner, it would seem), and was not to be eaten by the farmers. The first basket of figs was intended for the marquise, as were first-growth vegetables. Fruit is sweet and therefore supposedly the preserve of the masters. But it is also an agricultural product that tastes good to the farmworkers' children, too young to appreciate the importance of giving things up to those of higher social condition or caste. The ruling classes found that no attempt to reserve fruit for their special consumption could succeed.

In the rural world attempts to preserve fruit for winter supply were limited to drying apples and apricots and storing walnuts, almonds (in the Mediterranean), hazelnuts, and chestnuts, from which one could derive a sweet flour. Where the pine trees produced pignoli (pine nuts), the patience of the men assigned to shell them was rewarded by the high price of the product, though they had to be careful not to run into the owner of the pine grove, who, although he did nothing, felt entitled to an excessive share. The peasants were not stupid and knew how to avoid many such obstacles.

Dried fruit, available for consumption throughout winter, was a product rich in sugar that originated mostly in the southern Mediterranean. From the coast of Spain, where the Arabs were present until 1492, from Cyprus, and from the Greek islands and Mediterranean coasts of Africa and Asia Minor came cartloads of almonds, green or dried pistachio nuts, and dates—exotic and sweet items that spiced up more than one recipe. There were also the dried prunes shipped to Venice, Flanders, London, and Genoa whose name, *damaschine* (still used in Genoa today), reveals their Syrian origins.

The spread of sugar allowed Mediterraneans to export candied fruit, produced with the sugar "candy" that had nothing to do with Candia but was a particularly finely grained sugar produced in the Middle East. In the Early Modern era, when the Genoese for almost a full century held the hegemony of the production and marketing of sugar, fruit was preserved in jams and marmalades. Venice also took part in the sugar trade when in the fifteenth century Cyprus passed from Genoese to Venetian control.

Bitter oranges (cultivated in the western Mediterranean from the twelfth to the mid-nineteenth century) were made into marmalades. It is hardly a mystery that the English language labels *marmalade* the imported product made with citrus fruits and sugar and *jam* all other fruit conserves produced with locally raised fruit, sugar, and foodstuffs coming in from the colonies.

The western coast of Liguria, along with the Mediterranean coast of Spain, produced lemons and oranges from the twelfth century on. In the Early Modern era fruit products were exported to all countries in northern Europe, where lemons, lemon juice in containers, bitter oranges, and marmalade were also shipped.

Lemon production also took place on the banks of Lake Como, and the sale of these citrus fruits enriched a famous family that among other contributions gave the German Federal Republic a distinguished minister of foreign affairs: von Brentano.

The oranges from the Catalan coasts were called *toronja*, so the Sicilian oranges planted during the rule of Aragon and still produced today were called *tarocchi*. Whoever seeks documentation of the luxury status of lemons need only study the many Dutch still-life paintings from which lemons, among other luxury products, are never absent.

Salted or in brine, barrels of olives were shipped from Spain, Sicily, and Greece. Present on the banquet tables of the well-to-do, these large fruit were very much appreciated. Though somewhat expensive, they were popular: they appear on incoming bills of lading as well as the tax invoices of many Mediterranean port cities, where they were shipped either for local consumption or reexport to distant lands.

FIGURE 28
Lascivious banquet, seventeenth-century engraving by Martin de Vos.
(Milan National Historical Photo Collection)

CHAPTER ELEVEN

Fat Was Good

The consecrated oil for confirmation, ordination (including royal coronations), and extreme unction could only be olive oil. The oil that burned in the lamp devoted to the Host and Holy Sacrament had to be olive oil.

The limitations of olive culture are known to all: away from the plant the fruit does not ripen and therefore does not produce oil. But the tree also produces the leafy fronds that are consecrated or blessed for holy days. (The Hebrew tradition of cedars and palms was observed for many centuries thanks to the cedars and palms of San Remo and environs. San Remo was called "the city of palms" and provided them as needed both to the Hebrews who used them along with cedars in their Feast of the Tabernacle and to the pope in Rome on the occasion of Palm Sunday.) Olive trees were cultivated on church land wherever they would grow for use in rituals. From there the olive moved to the refectory tables of the abbeys and priories. This gave rise to a myth attributing the spread of olive culture to the Benedictines. As a result, the Benedictines were also credited with the invention of terracing (on the coastal strips of Liguria). Here I must interject that the Greek islands were all farmed in strips, that the Canaries were worked in terraces before the arrival of Europeans, and that Peru presented itself to the conquistadors already cultivated in strips. In Southeast Asia, moreover, it was not enough to cultivate hills and mountains by terracing alone: the strips were also flooded with water for rice farming.

The outreach of the Benedictines, though enormous, was not ubiquitous. Still, the learned brothers, though known by different names, had great merit both as agronomists and especially as jurists. They contributed to the extension of the use of the standard contract created by the legislators of Alessio, emperor of the Eastern Empire. This contract dealt with the relationship of the peasants to the land, ensuring that they did not become slaves in serfdom. With such a contract, which allowed for very low rents, one could ask the farmer to plant a few olive trees.

But the planting of olive groves intended for food supplies and for export was a mercantile phenomenon. During the fourteenth century in Tuscany, the concept of sharecropping already present in the thirteenth century spread. In Liguria the noble families expropriated Church properties and imposed a feudal culture. In both cases raising olives became obligatory. Oil could be exported at prices matching those commanded by large quantities of grain. It was no accident that the Venetians, in whose region only an insignificant quantity of oil was produced, required cultivation of olives on the Greek islands that came into their possession, from Corfu to Candia and Cyprus, to name only the largest. Oil was exported to the Germanic countries and for urban consumption elsewhere. The entire European coast of the Mediterranean produced olive oil: Greece, the Italian peninsula, Liguria, Andalusia (in great quantity from the era of Imperial Rome on), and later, Catalonia and Provence.

The sixteenth century saw an increase in oil production and its use for non-food-related purposes: growers produced oil for votive and household lamps, as well for the production of woolen cloth and manufacture of soap. In eighteenth-century Seville a soap factory was established, and even if it was under foreign ownership its production had be supplied with local oil. The Spaniards of Mexico, at least in the early days, imported olive oil from Andalusia for their requirements. The product was rather expensive, however, and its spread to the table of the people of the north and the remote hinterland seems insignificant. Other fats were used instead: some of negligible importance were limited to small areas of production; others, mostly animal fats, were more widely used. Since only olive oil results from pressings effected by purely mechanical means, seed oils had to await the invention of the chemical industry to enter the world of foods.

Frying in oil was perhaps limited to the Mediterranean. Far or not too far from the coasts frying was done in pork lard. In the Islamic lands fat from sheep or lambs' tails was used. I don't have enough data to cite this conclusively, but I imagine that use of the fat from sheep tails also spread to England, as well as to Spain on the lands belonging to the Mesta Company. The presence of millions of sheep must have convinced at least the poor to make use of this resource.

Pan for frying

Geese also provided a significant quantity of fat that came to be used both for cooking and for conserving goose meat, cooked and covered in its own fat. Animal fats seemed to be the most widespread, judging from both cookbooks and the livestock technical resources of different countries.

Butter came last. Though easily produced in large quantity, it was almost untransportable. In countries where production was significant it was heavily salted and could be shipped to distant consumers, but the fresh product could only travel short stretches, and the herds were usually far from the large cities. Of necessity, people turned to butter from nearby farms to prepare refined and sufficiently rich (short) dishes as well as to pursue the nascent art of pastry making, whose products were also very expensive.

For those living in the Alps with their own cows, butter was the available fat, produced with milk leftover from cheese manufacture (cheese was eminently transportable). The same held for the inhabitants of Denmark and Brittany. (It is in fact no accident that trout, Dover sole, and turbot are still cooked in butter.) But the demand from large cities in temperate or hot climates could not be fully satisfied. Butter long remained available only to those who could pay high prices, because production by the buttery farms near urban agglomerations was insufficient.

Everything that oozed fat was good. Rembrandt van Rijn and Peter Paul Rubens, not to mention Italian painters and thousands of others less known, sang a hymn to cellulite. Fat was beautiful. Just raise your eyes to the ceiling frescoes of almost all Italian Renaissance palaces, and you can admire lords and ladies, some quite young, plump as the puti angels in the churches or the cupids of country villas.

Favorable expressions using the adjective *fat* are innumerable all over Europe, as old as the figures of Dionysus and Silenus. Fear of hunger and famine was exorcised in depictions of thin and emaciated peasants (Dürer) and fat, hale, and hearty nobles and bourgeois. Some of these representations may have been ironic, but no doubt Rembrandt's Artemis (or Sophonisba) did not displease the client!

Gravy pan

FIGURE 29

Pepper and betel, engraving from Diderot and D'Alembert,
*Encyclopédie; ou, Dictionnaire raisonné des sciences,
des arts et des métiers* (The encyclopedia; or, Dictionary of
sciences, arts, and trades) (Paris, 1772).

CHAPTER TWELVE

Spices

The mania for spices ("la folie des épices," in the words of Fernand Braudel) was, along with market for silk and wool, one of the driving forces in medieval commerce. Doctors believed, wrote, and said that spices possessed therapeutic, digestive, and other powers, not the least being the aphrodisiac properties generally attributed to very pricey foods (oysters, shellfish, truffles, and saffron and other spices, to cite only a few).

When something is expensive, it quickly becomes one of the products that confer prestige. The ostentatious use of spices became a veritable obsession. As Cipolla recounts in his witty booklet *Allegro ma non troppo*, Europeans liked pepper, and for pepper they went so wild that it became a commodity of exchange and was used almost like money.

Pepper was the most important spice, and it has enjoyed great popularity since the end of the medieval period. Other spices have almost been forgotten, while cloves and nutmeg have resisted oblivion—always at high prices.

Whatever early doctors and historians said of them, spices have no real medicinal function. One cannot deny that they stimulate gastric juices and add to flavor, but the physicians at the end of the Middle Ages and in the Early Modern era, bound as they were by the precepts of Galen and other classics (the classic for a humanist comes close to dogma), were not trustworthy, and in the great majority of cases their medicine was actually harmful.

As for historians, sometimes they seem to concoct hypotheses solely to explain customs not reducible to logical origins. Their mania for codifying the why and wherefore of everything thus has induced them to write senseless treatises based on the pretext that spices were used in the conservation of food or at least helped in its preservation. But pickled meats exist without spices though flavored with garlic (in Provence); salt, drying, or smoking preserves food, not the spices used for flavoring, whether pepper or paprika. Spices may help mask the bad smells emanating from imperfectly conserved meat, but they were too expensive compared to meat (one could purchase fresh meat at popular prices) to use for this purpose, and besides pepper and the other spices were reserved for the tables of the wealthy, who could in any case afford the best meats. (An interesting sidelight: one of the spiciest recipes known is is for the preparation of lamprey, a fish delivered live to the kitchen.)

The quest for spices, sold during the whole medieval period (a millennium) by the Arabs, the Genoese, and the Venetians, along with some Catalan competitors, was the official justification for the Portuguese exploratory voyages along the African coast. That justification was no more than a pretext for the Portuguese to consolidate their security by attacking the Muslims in their own lands, thus cutting off the Arabs in order to reach the gold of Mali on the Atlantic beaches. In any case, the results were important: the Portuguese occupied the Cape Verde islands and, more to the south, San Tomé, an uninhabited island on which they immediately planted sugarcane.

When spices were finally imported in great quantity, Europeans no longer appreciated them or at least showed much-diminished interest. In Germany and especially in Poland spices were still widely distributed for many years, and at the end of the sixteenth century the German city-states still imported enormous quantities of saffron from Catalonia and, by way of Venice, from the Abruzzo.

Mortar

Genoa, Florence, and Venice continued to use Oriental spices despite the African and American substitutes that had become available. Meanwhile the French, who were poised to become the rulers of European culinary culture, had decided to reduce the use of spices almost to the point of abandoning them altogether. Perhaps this can be explained by the fact that in France all spices had to be imported from foreign countries. But it might be more plausible that the new tendency was the result of a desire to renovate culinary practices to make them more French. Whatever the reason, the eighteenth century saw the ascendance of a new cuisine that the nineteenth century made a source of national pride.

With time spices were reduced to an almost insignificant role in French recipe books. While it is true that the cuisine of these books was almost always more advanced than popular practice, they nonetheless established the fashion in cooking. Besides, the people had long learned to replace these too expensive ingredients with fragrant herbs from their *terroir*. Once removed from the culinary habits of the rich, the value of spices as a sign of conspicuous consumption diminished and so did their price.

It is interesting to note that the use of pepper persisted in the dishes of the Tuscan lower classes, as did cloves in certain Piedmontese dishes. But although the rural population hangs on to traditions over the long haul, when they are able to adopt the appurtenances of the rich these rustics turn to them as means of ostentation. What may no longer be articles of luxury for the powerful remain such for the peasants who acquire them through drudgery and labor and still accord them a share of luxury. Even when affordable by an ever-growing number of consumers, spices were nearly always expensive relative to other commodities, and if you wanted them you had to buy them: they don't sprout in the gardens and fields. So a peasant who used spices was showing that he had enough money available to buy them.

The exhausting life of the rural population may not necessarily have borne the imprint of hunger—sometimes the peasants could eat more if they wished—but they did chafe against the lack of money, not just to buy those objects they needed that were produced in the city and the country but to add to these something superfluous, even frivolous. As Gaston Bachelard observed (quoted by Braudel): "The conquest of the superfluous provokes a spiritual excitement superior to that of mastering the necessary. Man is a creature of desire, not of need." And Marcel Mauss wrote: "It is not in production that society has found its vital energy. The great promoter is luxury."

One can give up eating a chicken from one's own flock in order to sell it for a profit that permits the satisfaction of other desires. There is a Portuguese maxim that I later found repeated as far afield as the Ligurian and Piedmontese terri-

FIGURES 30 AND 31

Cloves and vanilla, engraving from Pierre Pomet, *Histoire générale des drogues* (General history of drugs) (Paris, 1694).

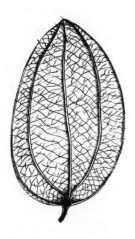

FIGURE 32

Nutmeg, engraving from Pietro Andrea Mattioli, *I discorsi* (Discourses) (Venice, 1568).

FIGURE 33

Cinnamon leaf, engraving from Michele Campi and Baldassare Campi, *Dialogo sul cinnamomo* (Dialogue on cinnamon) (1654).

tories: "When a poor man eats a chicken, one of the two is sick." The Portuguese version uses the word *pobre*; the Ligurian *villano*. I don't think this proverb is intended as a representation of poverty; rather, it reveals the widely held truth that desire is coin of the realm.

Spice "purse"

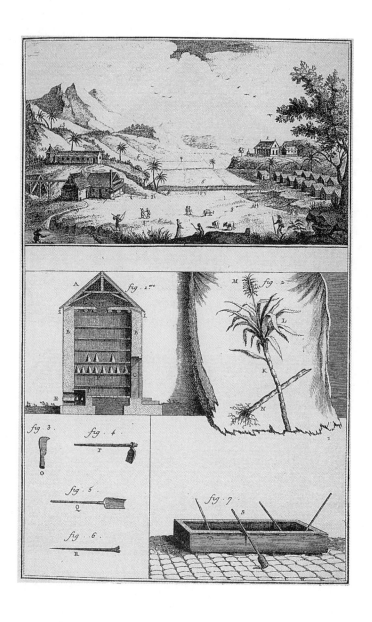

FIGURE 34
Sugar Mill, engraving from Diderot and D'Alembert,
*Encyclopédie; ou, Dictionnaire raisonné des sciences, des arts et des
métiers* (The Encyclopedia; or, Dictionary of sciences, arts, and
trades) (Paris, 1772).

CHAPTER THIRTEEN

The Atlantic, the East Indies, and a Few West Indies

If great historical events hardly seem to dent basic social structures, if people are almost never informed of the victories and names of military chieftains, they do not understand why so much misfortune comes to them. (Even when they do know, most prefer to close their ears to bad news.) It remains nonetheless true that the closing of the Dardanelles (or just the dangers of venturing there) and the conquest of the Greek, Venetian, and Genoese islands by the Turks, as well as their gradual conquest of the Balkan peninsula as far west as Hungary (with a small thrust to Vienna), convinced western Europeans to get their food supplies via alternative routes.

The Venetian possessions in the Greek islands became a serious burden for the *Serenissima* Republic, which defended them out of need and pride. The Genoese colonies in the Black Sea survived for a few decades, but no one would have invested a lira there. The Genoese turned toward Spain where, in Seville, more than three hundred merchants out of a total of five hundred were from Genoa (and these were among the richest). Others for some time had chosen Portugal and had undertaken the first Atlantic explorations.

The closing of easy access to Asia had important consequences, as did the occupation of the ensemble of Islamic countries by the Ottoman Turks, who often impeded and always complicated relations with westerners. The Portuguese tried to surround the Turks and to attack them on their Indian Ocean flank, but they ran up against serious military difficulties. And they also had trouble procuring spices—expensive products—which could be acquired from the East Indies or the Moluccas, bypassing the Arabian middlemen. This produced an upheaval in the market for the most expensive merchandise of that era: Lisbon became a trade center so full of pepper that the wholesale price collapsed. So too did the prices of other spices, including those found in Africa, which the French and English had come to appreciate as a source at least for a time, thanks to the distribution of spices undertaken there by the Dutch. The latter had a virtual shuttle going from Lisbon to Middleburg and then on to Amsterdam before they decided to replace the Portuguese on the African trade routes.

All this is meant to remind us that major historical events do count: the destruction of the "Invincible Armada" by the English and bad weather contributed not a little to the sea expeditions of the Dutch, who found themselves facing a notably weakened competitor on the high seas. The English and the Dutch were thus in a strong position to inflict punishment on their enemies; they also managed to take over the fishing banks that had been the proud entitlement of the Portuguese.

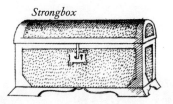
Strongbox

FIGURE 35
Gentleman and lady drinking chocolate, French engraving,
end of the seventeenth century.

CHAPTER FOURTEEN

From the Iberian Peninsula to the Distant Americas: The Sugar Route

If the Portuguese searched for spices and the Castillian hidalgos longed for El Dorado and, more realistically, to acquire manorial property that would yield them a title of nobility, Italian merchants cared mostly about land and its potential for productivity. Of course, they weren't averse to grabbing some letters of nobility for themselves. They knew, moreover, that the Atlantic islands would offer a climate suitable for the cultivation of sugar, so they supported the expedition of Christopher Columbus, who could count on the financial aid of many rich and influential fellow Italians in Seville.

In the sixteenth century Genoese interest in investing in sugar-seeking expeditions had already become a tradition. Without going into detail, a treaty of 1264 between the commune of Genoa and Philip of Montfort for free trade in Sur guaranteed the Genoese the use of public aqueducts for their sugar mills. Throughout the fifteenth century and well into the sixteenth, Genoese businessmen, determined to seek in the West what they had lost in the Levantine, had the sugar trade as one of their principal goals.

The history of the European settlements in the Canary

Islands was dominated by Genoese involved in sugar-related enterprises either directly on their own plantations or as financial investors, transporters, or merchants but always tightly and contractually linked to the local sugarcane farmers. In Madeira they won important privileges governing sugar exports. When dealing in sugar came, at least partially, to be reserved for Portuguese, the Genoese sought and obtained Portuguese naturalization papers, thereby continuing their lucrative trade.

Double sieves for spices and sugar

From the Lomellinis (Urbana and Battista) and Lodisio Doria, who already lived in villages on the Atlantic islands, Antonio Spinola obtained Madeiran naturalization on May 28, 1490. In 1500 Lorenzo Cattaneo obtained from the king of Portugal 50,000 *arrobas* of sugar (around 7,000 quintals); in 1503 Lazzaro Merello and his son Gio Batta formed a company for the marketing of Madeira sugar with the brothers Domenico, Bernardo, and Pantaleone from Sampierdarena. Similar examples could be cited for most of the sixteenth century.

In 1478 Christopher Columbus had landed on Madeira to seek sugar for the account of Paolo di Negro and Lodisio Centurione, the latter belonging to a long dynasty that lent its name to the whole history of the competitive race (or quest) for sugar. Columbus's first voyage led to the great discovery of the New World; on his second trip the admiral brought back with him sugarcane, planning to try to adapt it locally.

In Brazil the Centurione dynasty was among the pioneers from which would come the principal source of riches for that immense Portuguese colony and the basis of the decline of European sugar manufacture. In 1522, when Gaspare Centurione took the long sea route to Brazil to ensure continuation of his deceased brother Matteo's business, he transported among other things, as Charles de La Roncière put it, "a crafted metal apparatus composed of some fifty-five parts *to melt and refine sugar*, three thousand containers *to shape it*, with thousands of piles of bricks *to build the sugar mill*." Such technological commitment and well-defined economic goals created a strong demand for slaves and led, in Europe, to a radical transformation of the economics of sugar. From being a relatively expensive product, almost a spice or pharmaceutical, it soon became another foodstuff and replaced other sweeteners almost everywhere.

Given this, no one should be astonished that the sugar business enticed the nascent Dutch economic power to found soon thereafter a small colony in Curaçao and a larger one in Brazil. Holland equipped itself with refineries more modern than those in the Mediterranean: certainly more productive and able to create a prestigious international reputation, thanks also to chocolate (which I shall discuss in a few pages).

Nut and sugar graters

A variety of American products soon reached Europe: some were adapted; others were produced on-site by methods more rational than those used by the natives, thereby allowing for increased productivity. Among the first plants to spread to Spain and those parts of Europe controlled by the

Spanish crown (whose King Charles V was also emperor) was the *capsicum* (hot chili pepper), or *peperoncino*, which had amazing popularity and inflicted notable economic damage on the old spices. The empire's territory went from Cadiz to Budapest, bordering on Poland, including Lombardy and the kingdom of Naples, which facilitated the spread, among other goods, of *peperoncini* (hot peppers).

Capsicum circulated in all these countries under various names: *pimiento*, *peperone*, *spagnolino*, and paprika. With the unification of the crowns of Spain and Portugal under Philip II, the northern Moluccas, where Magellan had died, became the Philippines, and so the spicy, brightly colored plant invaded Asia, reaching as high as the peaks of the Himalayas.

This spread was certainly swift and surprising, but it is explainable by certain facts: (1) Chili peppers could be grown anywhere, in a pot or in the garden, and the plant cost almost nothing; (2) the "heat" provided by *peperoncini* was stronger than that of pepper, therefore its potency was greater; (3) *capsicum* was an exotic novelty that was also readily affordable; and (4) whoever could withstand the heat of the spice was deemed stronger (more *macho*). In the prosperous Italian and Dutch cities pepper resisted the onslaught of *peperoncini*, but from then on pepper's status as a symbol of wealth had come to an end.

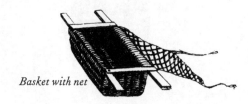

Basket with net

Along with *peperoncini* came beans, which reduced the European broad bean to the rank of a curiosity and spread quite rapidly, since people were already used to favas, pods, and other such vegetables, among them red-eye beans.

American beans, sturdier, more prolific, and thicker than those known in Europe, came to be used according to local traditions and ended up in soups and stews, partially replacing fava beans. Cooked European style with olive oil or bacon, they had great success and, because of their protein content, they helped to improve the diet of the less fortunate.

For the well-to-do classes there came the drink of the Aztecs: chocolate. Because sugar did not exist in America, the inhabitants of Central America drank a kind of bitter cocoa brew flavored with vanilla (called "Indian brew" by Piero Camporesi). In Spain, where the drink knew its first success among the most prominent families, sugar was soon used to sweeten it. Still, although known for generations, chocolate became popular (that is, reached an affordable price) only at the end of the nineteenth century, when first a Dutchman and later some Swiss succeeded in preparing it according to modern methods.

Copper cooker with tripod

From America came turkeys, which were quickly adapted and bred, first in the country houses of rich Spaniards and Genoese (the birds resembled peacocks) but soon also in the courtyards of dairy farms. Turkey hens reproduced in vast quantities, whereas the roosters were (and are to this day) subject to rigorous triage at the moment of sexual maturation. It is certain that one could buy turkeys ("roosters from India," as in the French *dinde*) in the shops of poultry retailers in Genoa as early as the second half of the sixteenth century. Their price was high compared to other farmyard poultry because of the exotic origins of the bird, but the price was soon adjusted, and turkey replaced goose and even capons on the Christmas tables of many Italians.

Of all the products from America turkey was the only one to succeed as a source of animal dietary protein. Even if farmhouses welcomed the guinea pigs that were found during the first explorations of India they never had much success as nourishment. With the exception of Newfoundland cod, which brought a major protein contribution to the European diet, America generally was a poor source of new protein. It is true that Aztec chiefs ate tapirs, but this was a privilege denied ordinary people, who also could not kill the rare cervids reserved for the chieftain. These animals were few in number and hard to capture, especially with the means available to the Mexican natives. A tapir on the king's table or else in a zoo is not even meat; a herd of cattle, a flock of sheep, or a herd of pig, on the other hand, is economically meaningful—it *is* meat, that is, merchandise.

Above all, Central America and much of the continent south of Mexico,(except for the western coastal strip (Peru and Chile), turned out to be sorely lacking in quadrupeds that might feed the natives and later the protein-needy conquistadors. The products emanating from the West Indies were mostly vegetal. Cocoa had enormous success but was not successfully adapted to local soil in Europe, so it had to be imported; so too did pineapple, which had so delighted the first explorers. The plants that did quickly adapt to European soil and climate and demonstrated the promise of a widespread popularity and distribution were zucchini gourds (*curcurbita pepo* and *curcurbita maxima*), which joined the traditional zucchini called "trumpet shaped." From green zucchini to gigantic yellow pumpkins the prolific breed became a widely accepted ingredient of many country

Meleagris en Grec, Gibber en Latin, Coc d'Inde en Francoys.

FIGURE 36

Turkeys, engraving by Belon du Mans, 1555.

FIGURE 37

Virginia Potato Plant, engraving from John Gerard, *Herbal* (1597).

dishes. The *solanaceae* also quickly took root: mid-six-teenth-century reports mention tomato and potato plants decorating botanical gardens in Spain and elsewhere.

The potato had to wait until the seventeenth century to be cultivated in Ireland, where it was so successful that it later caused a disaster. The Irish made of the potato a kind of monoculture, a lone national agricultural product. When the potato beetle (a coleoptera that attacks the tuber) destroyed the plantations, many Irish had to emigrate because the country was reduced to famine. In the rest of Europe it was not until the end of the eighteenth century—and in some locations not before the nineteenth—that people were per-suaded to feed themselves on the tuber of a plant that animals (quite justifiably) didn't want to eat! The tubers were used as pig fodder, in Prussia, for example, and in the eighteenth century the contemptuous Prussians fed them to their French prisoners. The French found them tasty, and Par-mentier, freed from prison, successfully convinced his com-patriots to dine on potatoes. Thwarted in their plan to pun-ish the French, the Germans decided to consume potatoes themselves, and in such quantities as to justify the use of "*Kartoffeln*" as a derisive name for Germans, much as Ital-ians are called "macaronis."

Potatoes did not quickly enter culinary consciousness because they were untranslatable, difficult to adapt for use in other foods, no matter what Battarra said of them in his dia-logues, where, he insisted that potato flour could be made into bread. There just did not exist enough cultural handles or referents to allow people to incorporate the potato into the corpus of their food, as had happened for beans or for the fava bean (which the Spaniards called *fabas*). In addition, the fruit of the potato can be poisonous, and unripe tubers are toxic. People needed time to find ways of using this food that today is an accepted staple.

As I have noted, the chili pepper was quickly welcomed

and assimilated, at least in name, to pepper. The same did not hold for the tomato, which remained primarily a decorative plant in gardens until the end of the nineteenth century, despite some attempts to reduce tomatoes to a sauce to flavor or season meats. Nevertheless, tomatoes met with a modest welcome in the Mediterranean world, though they were eaten only raw in salads, and then only beginning in the early eighteenth century. For their transformation into sauce and their ascendancy as one of the preferred foods of the Mediterranean population one had to wait for the nineteenth century, which is beyond the chronological purview of this book.

I can, however, reaffirm without subverting my stated topic that the use of the tomato had its first successes in Catalonia, Provence, and western Liguria, from whence it passed into the Piedmont and Emilia before becoming so decisively a characteristic food of Campania.

This is a good opportunity to go into the details behind a fact already mentioned here: the first imported tomato and the first and oldest reference to the plant were curiosities without relevance for food history. A plant in a botanical garden is a spectacle, an object for study. Pineapples, pepperoni, corn, and potatoes, in contrast, were products that affected the economy and became food resources.

One plant, however, did enjoy extensive popularity in the early modern period: corn. Described with precision by Michele da Cuneo (from Savona) in a valuable account written on the occasion of Christopher Columbus's second voyage, corn was linked to maize, or Indian corn (sorghum), by the similar shapes of the two plants. Da Cuneo was the first to call it *mais* (corn), and, by like analogy, this is also what the Piedmontese peasantry called it. Corn arrived first in Spain, and in the first years of the sixteenth century it was grown in Andalusia, Catalonia, and Castille and later in Portugal, France, and Italy, as well as southern Hungary and the Balkans. It seems that corn entered the Veneto, by various

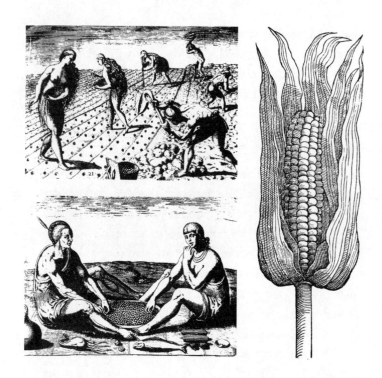

FIGURE 38
Cultivating corn, engraving from Lemoyne de Morgues, *Brevis nar-
ratio eorum quae in Florida Americae provincia Galis acciderunt* (Short
history of those who came to Florida in America from provinces of
France) (Frankfurt/Main, 1591, 1609).

FIGURE 39
Corn (a.k.a. Turkish grain), engraving from Giovan Battista
Ramusio, *Navigazioni e viaggi* (Travels and voyages)
(Venice, 1565).

routes from Spain, in first half of the sixteenth century. Since it was treated as a foreign product, corn took on the exotic name par excellence: *granturco* (Turkish grain). This name was also adopted in Tuscany, whose transactions with the Venice *la Serenissima* were at the time frequent and cordial. The corn in question was of the white variety, which was very popular and is still used, finely ground, to make a white polenta to serve with fish, game, and meat.

Francesco Carletti, one hundred years after its discovery, visited America—henceforth a Spanish colony—and came across maize. He knew it well from Tuscany as *granturco*, but he did not succeed in appreciating the local food traditions. Nor did he appreciate tortillas, longing for bread instead of toasted corn.

In Italy corn was eaten and prepared as polenta, formerly made with sorghum. In Croatia, Slovenia, and Bosnia one made polenta with corn the same way the Greeks made it with yellow bean flour. The possibility of adapting corn to European food traditions was the determining factor in its spreading popularity. Of course, the crisis in agriculture that beset Europe in the seventeenth century convinced many farmers and peasants to overcome old prejudices.

At first, broken ears of corn were given to animals, but in the seventeenth century the vassals of the imperial feudal lords, often mercantile, entrepreneurial nobility, quickly recognized that this new, very prolific product could be used to feed the poor farmer. Corn was a product easily grown in the short term, and the harvest could be left for the farmer to feed his own family, thereby permitting the landowner to claim a larger share of the wheat crop. These vassals thus lost no time in convincing their peasant subjects to feed themselves on the same corn that on the landlords' country estates was intended for the farm animals. Polenta left the kitchen garden to become an agricultural crop, and corn began its agricultural integration and assimilation with local soil and traditions.

The peasants began to resist the development of corn cultivation when they realized that from then on this novelty would have to be consigned to the landowner and belong to the category of taxed crops. Different agricultural traditions, the presence of small landholdings, and the variety of crops grown saved the people of Monferrato from a diet based almost entirely on polenta. In other countries, where the balance of agriculture was different and the contractual arrangements harsher, the deficiency in niacin made its effects known with the pellagra epidemic that began in northern Spain around 1730 and spread to France, the Balkans, and northern Italy, where it lingered until the first decades of the twentieth century.

America also yielded other plants of less prominence. The Jerusalem artichoke, whose big yellow-petaled blossoms festooned the banks of rivers, has an edible root that was and still is combined with other greens in delightful dishes (*bagna cauda*, for example). Other gigantic yellow flowers served only to decorate gardens until, in the first decades of the eighteenth century, people learned how to extract oil from sunflower seeds. This led to a major expansion of sunflower cultivation in northern European countries (France, Germany, England, Russia), which lacked the resource of olive groves.

Cactus was imported to shelter the ladybug, an insect that yields a red dye. When one dyed with aniline, one no longer had to deal with the plant's awkward fruit. Prickly strawberries were adapted but slow to gain popularity. Imported from North America they suffered compared to produce from Central and South America.

Medicinal plants were imported, such as quinine, used in Rome and Genoa by the Genoese doctor Sebastiano Baldo (or Blado), who in the middle of the seventeenth century was head doctor at the Hospital for Incurables in Genoa. Also imported were trees for timber, ornamental plants, and tobacco, but these are not foods.

The peoples of the conquered countries had mores very different from those of Europeans. Warriors and chieftains acquired protein for themselves through war; everyone else had to turn to animals that were not always inviting. Europeans didn't want to stay in the Antilles or Mexico if they had to taste and perhaps eat everything there just to survive. It became necessary therefore to supply America with the plant and animal products it lacked that could adapt to the new environment.

Big soup spoon

FIGURE 40
Conquistadors in the New World, engraving from
Historia Americae (History of America) (Frankfurt/Main, 1602).

CHAPTER FIFTEEN

From Europe to America

Michele da Cuneo wrote to the nobleman Geronimo Aymari, member of a family of Ligurians traveling in Seville and other Spanish cities. The scribe copying the letter misspelled the family name as "Annari," so for a long time no one could trace the addressee, not even I, who relied for a time on the manuscript copy. Geronimo Aymari was a merchant who knew Columbus and sponsored the voyage of Michele da Cuneo in exchange for reliable and possibly true information. The news bulletins sent were dated October 28, 1495.

The high-blown rhetoric usually used to exalt the exploits of Columbus is absent from Michele da Cuneo's narrative, and there is no talk here of earthly paradise. The author simply reported what he saw; he was not a humanist but a businessman. From the newsletter of this traveler from Savona and from some passages by Francesco Carletti, another writer-merchant who arrived in America a century after its discovery, I have derived the documentation necessary to support the remarks that follow.

The impact of European produce in the Antilles and on the American continent was stronger than that of American products in Europe and much more quickly felt. Already during his first voyage Christopher Columbus found that the newly discovered islands, while abundant in fish and birds, were all but devoid of four-legged animals. Grains such as corn had not yet won over anyone, and the other foodstuffs did not allow for a diet up to European standards. "They seem to me to be cold people, not too libidinous, which may be because they eat badly," wrote Michele da Cuneo. His observations contrast with the celebratory remarks of those who wrote to gain attention or were enjoined to praise the heroic undertaking.

I shall now compare the writings of Cuneo and a letter by Angelo Trevisan, who was very thorough but nevertheless wrote to hear himself talk and copied the work of Pietro Martire d'Anghiere, compiled later in Spain:

This plain is so fertile that in the gardens cultivated on the banks of the river are sown various kinds of greens such as radishes, lettuce, cabbage. Only sixteen days after seeding all plants blossomed and were ripe. Melons, watermelons, pumpkins, gourds, zucchini, and others were harvested thirty-six days after seeding, and never has one tasted better. Sugarcane took fifteen days. They even say the second year after new planting perfect grapes were produced. A peasant to test whether this land could produce grain sowed seeds in early February and by mid-March the ears of wheat were ripe. The straw was thicker, the sheaves longer, and the grain better than ours and than any I have ever seen.

(Angelo Trevisan)

To inform you the better we brought with us from Spain various seeds and seedlings that we planted to test which would grow well and which badly. Those that did well are the following: spring melons, watermelons, various radishes, and gourds. The others, such as onions, lettuce, leeks, and other salad greens, did poorly and are very small except the hand-grown plants, which yield the best product.

The grains measured ten days later grew inch by inch and might easily and suddenly fall or dry out.

(Michele da Cuneo, letters 33A and 34)

It seems to me that these two descriptions are their own commentary. But Michele da Cuneo adds one remark: "The soil is black and fertile, but they haven't yet found the way nor the time to sow properly. The fact remains that no one wants to live in these countries." The author makes similar and very interesting observations on animals (letter 34): "The fact of it remains that very few are found on these islands. The Lord Admiral brought the most necessary of them from Spain. We have found first-rate pigs, chickens, dogs, and cats produced here. Especially outstanding in quality are the pigs because of the great abundance of fodder (good for porkers). Cows, horses, sheep, and goats behave as they do in our country."

Coffeepot

On his second voyage Columbus had planned to bring plants and animals, though not of course because he had foreseen the unification of the world economy (he did not even realize that he wasn't in Asia). He saw, however, that the islands suffered from major deficiencies in protein nutrients, if one excepted fish, which Europeans tended to view as reserved for lean days and in any case considered low in nutritional value. The goal was to provide Europeans who landed in the Caribbean islands with a diet similar to that of their homelands. This had political implications, seeing that with the exception of the most merciless and ferocious of the Caribs, the natives had for some time given up their canni-balistic practices, which were alleged mostly to justify deceptive and abusive actions by the Europeans.

With the conquests of Mexico and Peru the Europeans found themselves confronted by advanced civilizations cul-turally far more evolved than that of the Caribs and Arawaks. They also found stags, mountain lions, tapirs, and many other animals, such as the lama, alpaca, and guanaco. During these same years Cabral took over Brazil for the Portuguese. After a few years, the cultivation of sugarcane, which at first seemed not to take hold (perhaps expectations were excessive), spread wherever it was possible. Entire "buildings for sugar" (factories) were brought over from Europe and provided a strong incentive for the slave trade. Slavery in the sugar fields was a horrible example of eco-nomic unification, but it was an almost unique phenomenon, to which one might add, if to a far smaller degree, the culti-vation of cocoa and coffee.

The Europeans sought to reproduce in the New World both the traditional diet of their homelands and the very language of food. They also introduced there pigs, cows, sheep, goats, horses, donkeys, chickens, and pretty much everything that was bred and raised in the Old World. The rapid acclimatization or adaptation to local conditions of wheat, grapevines, and olives (in Peru) reestablished in America the ancient Mediterranean dietary habits, over-whelming, rather too easily, local food culture and tradi-tions. Still, from that culture emerged products like cocoa, which Europeans knew how to transform into what we call chocolate by adding butter derived from the cocoa itself

FIGURE 41
Work on a plantation, engraving from the end of the
eighteenth century.

and sugar produced from imported cane. Other native products grafted onto the transplanted Mediterranean cuisine were hot peppers (which figured in almost all the Spanish dishes in Mexico), beans, bell peppers, pineapple, and other fruit.

Along with the imported and adapted food products, the wheel and iron came to America. This led to an enormous increase in productivity. For example, cultivating corn with manure fertilizer and the plow produced greater yields; the same held true for potatoes.

Other changes resulted from the introduction of a population originating on another continent, with more efficient weapons and organization, with an incomprehensible culture, bearers of lethal diseases for a population lacking natural immunity to them. Then too the Europeans brought a religion that preached love that did not admit toleration of any kind, and under whose sign people and villages were burned. The result for the people of South and Central America was a disaster one could well label genocide, at least for the Arawak, the Caribs, and, two hundred years later, for the Indians of North America. The Europeans too caught diseases that were new to them and spread these throughout the world.

Pan

When Francesco Carletti (a Florentine slave trader) visited these countries around a hundred years after Michele da Cuneo, he found Spanish dominion well entrenched, though at times entwined with some local traditions. Most of the products that Carletti found had names in the languages of the various European countries and sometimes even in regional dialects.

When Carletti had to turn to corn because bread was lacking he complained: "Living very uncomfortably and with extreme need of anything vital for life, especially of bread, which no one could procure and in replacement of which we ate what the Indians prepare with corn that we call *grano di Turchia*." This is yet further confirmation that in Tuscany at the end of the sixteenth century corn was well known and had taken on the popular name of *granturco*. In contrast, potatoes were still a novelty to Carletti; he mentions "in particular certain tubers called 'potatoes,' which boiled or roasted under a fire have a delicious taste as pleasant as our chestnuts and which can replace bread."

Carletti also notes that iron weapons were brought from Europe and describes with a wealth of detail the trade in slaves from Africa and their sale in America, specifying the taxes and rates and contrasting the prices in Mexico to the higher ones obtained in Peru.

His description of the alpaca shows him to be careful. He recognizes it as belonging to the *Camelidae* species, even if the Spaniards confuse it with the ram: "[These are] beasts of burden native to this country; the Spaniards quite improperly call them *carneros*, that is, rams, but the Indians call them pack horses and from those I saw for sale it struck me that they resembled tiny camels (except for their lack of hump) because their neck, head, and feet were just like those of camels, but of course less strong and much smaller. Their meat is good to eat, and the Indians make clothes from their wool."

Carletti's book is a temptation to plagiarism, but instead I conclude with two observations that justify my comments here and clear the field of "economic plan" hypotheses. Perhaps five hundred years ago one might have been inclined to think that whatever happened was part of a plan, but this is not true. Unification did not happen then, nor was it completed even in our time. All that happened was that Europeans settled in America. Many of them became rich, indeed very rich, and had sent from Europe for their personal consumption not only foods but articles of luxury. Gold and silver, sugar, cocoa, cotton, and even slaves were items of exchange between the Europeans of Europe and those of America.

Tripod

At the time of Hernán Cortés, the Castillian crown forbade the planting of vines and olives in New Castille. The purpose of the interdict is clear, but let us see what F. Carletti wrote on the subject: "This country [Mexico] lacks grapes, therefore wine, and oil, because the king does not wish the earth to be cultivated. That would, he knew, produce and lead to vines and olives as good as those in our European countries. The king wants wine and oil to come here from Spain, since these products have brought limitless treasure to his customs and to his vassals." But this edict did not extend to Peru, which produced and exported oil and wine: "So much wine was harvested that there was not only enough for the needs of this country but enough to satisfy Mexico and other places. . . . And there is no need for it to be brought from Spain from where it was sent at incredible cost and at great inconvenience, since wine had to be transported from one sea to another on muleback in earthenware jugs."

Wherever possible, as in Lima, the Spaniards re-created their society, if much more opulently. In Lima they seized all the silver coming from Potosí, where thousands of Indians worked sustained by coca. The ostentatious display of riches even extended to the clothing worn by the slaves: "On feast days it is amazing to see these Negroes going superbly adorned in garments of silk, with pearls and with jewels. . . . Even more astonishing is the sight of the majesty and splendor of the attire of the Spanish wives and in other gestures that express vainglory."

Only the Spanish enjoyed such great wealth, although vanity induced them to extend its benefits to some of their African slaves. There were also a very few wealthy natives, those who had freed themselves from the Aztec yoke only to submit to working under European domination. But little was left over for the other Indians, who either fought colonization from the forests—as did those Carletti called "Criumechi"—or survived on the margins of this wasteful society, where the cost of living had become very high and natives were forced to do the work that Spaniards refused to do. Above all they were to fish, "being that the Spaniards were horrified at doing something so vile." This attitude has done more than a little harm to the nutritional culture of countries under Spanish domination, where specifically fishing and fish did not enjoy popularity.

In Peru and in Mexico there was disembarked merchandise from China, as well as from all the American countries, including slaves shipped from Angola. Whatever arrived in Peru was paid for with silver from Potosí:

> What merchandise and goods arrived with the Spanish ships were consumer goods and necessities exclusively for the Spaniards, not for the Indians as many thought. The times were no longer those of the natives' early richness and simplicity, thanks to which the first Spaniards who went there, in exchange for trifles such as bells, mirrors, ironware, knives, glass beads, and similar knickknacks, extracted their gold and silver. Then by force of arms they took possession both of the land and of its people. Now the Spaniards alone taste the pleasures of the country.

As did, Carletti continues, "the merchants who loaded the ships that go from Spain to the Indies with such varied goods, affordable because of the millions in gold seized from the hands of the Indians."

To the Indians were left only the new diseases that decimated them:

> In this country they are declining fast. . . . Many of them are dying off. . . . After having been rather ill they dropped dead, a misfortune that concerned only them, not the Spaniards who through the bad treatment they inflict are the cause of things ending that way. . . . Instead of giving them money in payment (after having worked and provided victuals) they curse them and do them harm. So through this and other inhuman treatments God allows their death, and within a short time it is thought that all perished as happened on the island of San Domingo, which was heavily populated at the time of Columbus's discovery and is now deserted and without inhabitants.

Within less than a hundred years the mines of Potosí swallowed up tens of thousands of men, and diseases destroyed huge numbers of them. Mistreated and deprived of land and dignity, condemned by the Inquisition for their religious practices, the Indians of Central America fled to the forests, where they resisted for a long time but were nevertheless destined to succumb.

The Indians of North America did not fight against the Spaniards but did not meet a kinder fate as a result. Rather, they were stripped of their lands and starved out by men to whom monuments are now erected, such as Buffalo Bill, who dedicated himself with skill and selflessness to the systematic destruction of wild buffaloes, the unique economic resource of the prairie Indians and their main food source.

It took five hundred years for the ideas of Las Casas to have a modest impact, and even today we witness deception and destruction. The examples of Amazonia and Chiapas are hidden from view and denied the general spotlight they deserve.

Double prongs

Still, the acclimatization of so many meat-producing animals and the introduction of the wheel, the plough, and iron brought to America an enormous quantity of protein and improved agriculture and farming, reducing hunger and backbreaking work among the survivors of the genocide—especially backbreaking work (think of men moving along impassable trails, transporting essentials on their backs). Even so, it would take many, many years before these peoples, who only now are slowly beginning to increase in numbers, could hope for real integration and the rebirth of their dignity.

It took the industrial revolution to produce the most important effects of economic integration between Europe and America. Refrigerator ships brought to Europe meat from Argentina, cotton from America, wheat from Canada, and even pineapple and bananas from the West Indies. After the Second World War, the products of U.S. technology came to Europe in such quantity as to create a platform capable of sustaining a cultural invasion. Only now can one speak of efforts at integration or globalization, efforts that European culture can turn to its advantage.

Bellows

FIGURE 42
Banquet to mark Joseph I's accession to the imperial throne,
engraving by J. C. Hackhofer, 1705.

CHAPTER SIXTEEN

To Eat at the Same Mensa

When the harpy cursed Aeneas she prophesied such extreme hunger for the hero and his companions that "they would bite even into the *mensa*." The prophecy revealed itself less terrible than it had at first appeared. Aeneas and his men found themselves eating even the round disks of bread the handmaidens distributed at the beginning of banquets that were used like plates (although, given their status as noble warriors, they knew they were being humiliated). The companions of the son of Venus thereby ate the oldest pizza in history. Soaked in the juices of the foods that were placed on them to be sliced, these disks of bread were called *mensa(e)*.

Each *mensa* was used by two people, who therefore "ate at the same *mensa*," cutting the meats placed on the bread. As early as the twelfth century, long before other countries, the bread *mensa* (or sliced bread) was replaced in Italy by a *tagliere*, or cutting board, a disk made of wood or terra-cotta, often seen in medieval documents, that was shared by two diners. At the end of the fifteenth century, *stare a tagliere* (be at the cutting board with someone) had the same meaning as "to share the same table." From the fifteenth century, however, and in Italy before anywhere else, the use of individual plates, separate glasses, and, as already recounted, the fork had become widespread. (Jean-Louis Flandrin writes that in France the large bread slices were replaced by plates only beginning in the sixteenth century.)

Heating pan for food, with its tiles

Humanism had had its impact. I do not mean that this whole revolution grew out of the writings of the humanists, but at the least the new customs and manners born in the world of the city-states found their expression in a new way of seeing and perceiving: for example, the notion of the individual point of view, which justifies the use of perspective, understood here as the point of view of the observer (of a painting, for instance).

The set and laid table encouraged the proliferation of crockery and dinnerware made of gold and silver for the very rich, of pewter and fine pottery for the prosperous bourgeoisie, of wood and shoddy ceramics for those with less purchasing power. From the end of the fifteenth century onward, paintings show banquets far more luxurious and elaborate than those shown in medieval frescoes. There are plates and underplates in front of each guest, with at least one glass per person, and bottles placed on the table (goblets and bottles were made of glass).

All this incited potters to perfect their art in order to produce less and less porous ceramics, initially by using rough glazing, later by covering glazes with a vitreous skin, and gradually developing ever more sophisticated techniques. Comparing

FIGURE 43
Proposal for a Dinner and Table Setting for Thirty-two Guests,
engraving from V. Corrado, *Il cuoco galante* (The gallant cook)
(Naples, 1786).

fourteenth-century ceramics (setting aside Byzantine, Persian, and some Arabic products) with those produced during the fifteenth century in Paterna, Malaga, and Majorca and later by the masters in Faenza and elsewhere offers evidence of extraordinary creative production and dizzying technical progress.

Glass and ceramic factories diversified their product lines, for the kitchen or for the table, for pharmacies or perfumeries (my concern here is the kitchen, of course). With the passage of time, from the seventeenth to eighteenth century, the ever more crowded table will support myriad objects, intended for sauces, salads, broth or soup, meat, fish (this one large, that one small), snails, shellfish, fruit (which had to be served in a special fruit bowl), foie gras, pâté, rillettes, salt, pepper, bread, and hard and soft-boiled eggs in their special ceramic eggcups, which would be replaced in the 1820s by porcelain eggcups produced in Bohemia. While plates might be of gold and silver, salad bowls had to be made of ceramic or porcelain, half-moon shaped as though to emphasize that salad is a mere accompaniment.

Before the discovery of the kaolin caves in Germany, the English and Dutch had manufactured in China the porcelain objects that today antique dealers call "East India Company." The Genoese and Venetians, as early as the sixteenth century, produced entire table services in ceramic, decorated with white and blue Chinese motifs or else with dark blue patterns set against a light blue background. The table settings imitated Ming Dynasty porcelain and came to be sold everywhere in Europe. They were considered artistic bric-a-brac but sold well throughout Europe.

The obligation of the master of the house and of the serving staff to know how to use all this equipment correctly became acute with the popularity of chocolate, which was served in special bowls called cups. Francesco Carletti men-

FIGURE 44
Wedding banquet, engraving by Martyn van Meytens, 1736.

tions "bowls that they [the Mexicans] called chicchere." In fact, the word was *sikalli*, and this meant "little gourd bowls." The Spaniards interpreted this as *xícara* or *jícara*. Bowls for chocolate had to be a shaped rather differently from usual cups, as was the case for tea, which had its own specially designed service, and, later, for coffee. For each service, one had to think of an appropriate sugar bowl and provide a small pitcher for milk to be added to tea or coffee. Every liquid had its special vessel. Those of high birth received training sufficient to allow them to orient themselves among this plethora of utensils and glassware; others did not and thereby gave proof of their inferior breeding.

Glassware was no less impressive. If in Murano world-renowned works of glass art were produced, in Altare in Liguria bottles and glasses were produced in quantity. Master glassmakers went to work in France for noble families. Artisans from Altare furnished their employers with very elaborate cups and glasses and in return were richly rewarded both financially and with patent letters of nobility.

The manufacturers of tablecloths and napkins, especially those from Flanders, also did not fail to derive profit from this revolution of the customs of the table. First preceded and later imitated by the Italians, they marketed their fine and delicate linen creations throughout the world.

The reevaluation of changing table settings made the fortunes of potters, glassmakers, makers of tablecloths, and last but not least of silversmiths, who produced new services in sterling for the courts, the nobles, and the very wealthy. When Gio Francesco Brignole went as ambassador to Paris between 1736 and 1738, he asked Ballin, principal goldsmith of the king, to craft for him a complete table service in silver. Using the primary materials furnished him by Brignole himself (who had brought them from Genoa), Ballin fashioned table settings in the French style.

The mistress of the house, however, could not supervise

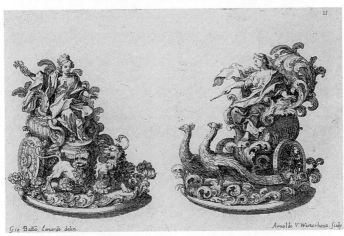

FIGURES 45 AND 46
Four ornamental stands of sugar, engraving from John Michael
Wright, *Ragguaglio della solenne comparsa* (Report from a
solemn guest) (Rome, 1687).
(Rome, Collection of the Casanatense Library).

every detail. Whether one or several, they tired quickly, so they had to turn over more and more tasks to the servants, training young men and women from the lower classes in the complexities of table service. The kitchen staff also required training to learn the job of head cook and to understand how to negotiate the various complex operations of an often numerous kitchen brigade.

Dining room servers and kitchen staff, serving at the table of the masters, learned table manners but above all learned to cook. They discovered that by using less expensive raw materials and strong herbs rather than spices they could prepare a rich man's dishes in a poor man's house. Their efforts also pleased the well-to-do, who went to taste these dishes in the taverns or had them served at home: polenta served on a silver platter became worthy of the master of the house and his table companions.

As the equipment for the table changed, so did the syntax of the meal, which gave up salad as first course. It was replaced by a "starter" that for a time in Tuscany was called *camangare*, that is, *capo del mangiare* (beginning or head of the meal), and in Liguria and other regions was *incisame* (cut into), where it meant *incominciame* (beginning). The word in Italian is awful, but the the phoneme *in*—as in *in*cominciare, *in*cidere, and so on—is significant: it is not *salata* that conveys the meaning but *in*-. When the word becomes *saleggiata* in some spoken dialects, more than one aspiring philologist has thus been deceived.

From the point of view of nutrition, the medieval custom of beginning with salad, still practiced in some Ligurian and Provençal families, was an excellent choice. But the French style, perhaps poorly understood, found it more elegant to serve salad as a side dish, even if with roasted meats, with the result that the whole was less digestible.

For the northern peoples salad was a food or cud for ruminants. Such a statement may arouse some ire, but in the

'60s the greengrocers of the northern cities, including Paris, were scarcely inviting. Among the innumerable offerings meat dominated, *la viande*, the vital food par excellence, and even fish was fresher than the greens, now relegated to the rank of side dish. A curious footnote: the first cauliflower reached Berlin thanks to Francesco Cirio (at the end of the nineteenth century).

Beef was relatively available in the Early Modern period, so even though it was much appreciated, one had to seek out better meats—game, for example—that had the merit of being rare, therefore expensive.

Another custom that ended was the serving of an almond and pine nut cake at the beginning of the meal, accompanied by a strong Malvasia wine. Throughout Europe more or else everyone bowed to the customs of France, which from the beginning of the eighteenth century until the twentieth exercised an unparalleled cultural hegemony over Europe. At the court of Saint Petersburg they spoke French, and in Vienna the language of diplomats (at least the written language) was French.

It seems that the service, that is, the sequence of dishes, was flexible even in France (according to Jean.-Louis Flandrin), and to honor a foreign custom established throughout Europe France finally adjusted to the modern sequential order of service that is called "*à la russe*." Prototypical menus from the doctors and magistrates who regulated consumption to limit excess—they were for meals destined for the hungry—dating from the first period of the Early Modern era are not yet ordered completely "grammatically." That "grammar" was still uncertain, and especially in Italy the complications of the Baroque period were an obstacle to the innovations that French cuisine tried to impose. Still, there existed in Italy some pockets of reasonableness, labeled niggardly by all, that guided taste in that country, the most prosperous in Europe at the end of the eighteenth century. I am speaking of daily, widespread consumption: people need to learn to smile at courtiers and their exaggeration. Four hundred years have passed since the civil war that brought Cromwell to power in England, and three hundred since the French Revolution. There is no longer any reason to regret or imitate court customs and their petty ethics.

*Container for kitchen
sideboard*

FIGURE 47
Pouring wine (wine bar), French engraving, end of
the eighteenth century.

CHAPTER SEVENTEEN

Eating and Drinking

The wealthy classes throughout all Europe drank wine at the table. The poor, in contrast, drank whatever beverage their homeland produced. That drink was wine in a region that extended as far as the northern limits of viticulture; it was beer or cider beyond that limit.

From the time of Eleanor of Aquitaine, England imported wine from the Bordeaux area. Sweet wine from Liguria and Campania came to Flanders in the north. The Hanseatic cities drank Mediterranean sweet wine. Southern Germany produced excellent wine, and all the other European countries produced wine wherever possible. Of course, in the Early Modern period other drinks, such as tea, coffee, and chocolate, also gained popularity. Taking tea became a widespread habit in those countries that did not produce wine, but at the table one drank wine whenever possible. The Buddenbrooks family of Lübeck described in Thomas Mann's novel drank malmsey and looked down on the Bavarians as beer drinkers.

The vine and wine, wrote Fernand Braudel, are products of civilization, just as the tea of the Chinese and Japanese is the sign of their special culture. If the world of Islam adopted tea because of religious prohibition and if other countries adopted it as a daily beverage because wine was too expensive for them (as in the northern countries, or Russia, where the samovar became the symbol of home and hearth), it is also true that many a noble table in Moscow and London displayed bottles of wine: a sweet gentle wine, pleasing to the palate, very different from the rough wine, or plonk, destined for workers or army troops.

For the Austro-Hungarian emperor and the princes of the realm, northern Hungary produced sweet Tokay according to the labor-intensive methods then in use. In France the marquis of Saluzzo, by now without a fiefdom, married the countess of Lur. Together they worked to produce the best sauternes in the world at Château d'Yquem. The German Rhineland states also produced sweet wines, the *Auslese*, for example, intended for aristocratic mouths. The czar of Russia had available to him the sweet wine produced in the Crimea by processes similar to those used for Tokay. The Dutch planted vines to produce sweet wine in South Africa, the Capetown wines, which they exported to Europe. Finally, the English, with the agreement concluded by Lord Methuen, pushed for production of sweet wine in Portugal (where Madeira already existed) and transformed the wines of Porto into a sweet wine, as had been done with Marsala in the nineteenth century. The English also acquired property in the Jerez della Frontera area and there produced Sherry, reaching the highest levels of perfection after their purchase of the Pedro Domecq holdings in Jerez. Italy produced "Greek" wine in Campania and muscatel in Piedmont. Ordinary wines were produced everywhere.

A frequently used process that yielded a product of lesser quality (called forced, crushed, and squeezed wines) but avoided loss of the harvest because of all too frequent unforeseen rains involved reducing the influx of juice, or sap, by pressing small grapes and then drying them on a mat.

Red wines tended to be sweet, at least those few saved by the peasants for feast days. But red wines were mostly meant for general consumption and like dry white wines obtained by inefficient processes they soon turned to vinegar or became dregs and undrinkable (for us today).

The habit of drinking sweet wines goes back at least to the thirteenth century, and it was Italian mercantile culture that helped spread the taste for these wines. Sweet wine contained sufficient sugar and alcohol and could be transported. The existence of grape species like the Spanish *garnacha* (*grenache* in France, *guarnaccia* in eighteenth-century Piedmont, *vernaccia* in ordinary Italian and in medieval Latin, where the two initial sounds are linked to form one, with *gua* becoming *v* ["Walter" is the same as "Gualtiero," *guado* the same as *vado*, etc.]) throughout Italy, France, and Spain afforded vintners the possibility of producing and transporting sweet and liqueur-like Grecian or Greek-style wines. Barbatelle, for example, was adaptable and could thrive in Campania. The taste for these wines was also encouraged by dedicated mercantile organizations, as happened for Santorini wine. First commercialized by the Venetians, who held that Greek island at the time, Santorini was then imitated in the province of Tuscany and elsewhere (the Venetians called it *vinsanto*, and soon *vinsanto* became a "local" product).

I do not wish to bore you any longer. The examples are limitless and so are the unacknowledged misappropriations of the names of better wines. One thinks of Tocai from Friuli, which is not the Hungarian Tokay, of the Dolcetto the Piedmontese peasants often call "Nebiolo," of so many Vernaccias distributed everywhere and unfortunately believed to be regional and local by so many misguided critics. When you say of a good wine, "This is a Tokay," a wine for royalty, or else "This is a Vernaccia," the wine runs in streams in the land of milk and honey. All these labels con-

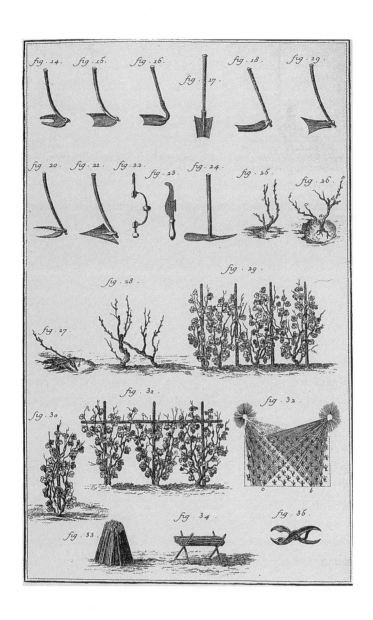

FIGURE 48

Agriculture. Vine Cultivation (Viticulture), engraving from
Diderot and D'Alembert, *Encyclopédie; ou, Dictionnaire raisonné
des sciences, des arts et des métiers* (The encyclopedia; or, Dictionary of sciences, arts, and trades) (Paris, 1772).

tribute to creating a fair amount of obfuscation. This confusion is fed by a lack of precise attention to the particular grape varietals paid by certain writers (Sante Lancerio and Bacci, to mention only two of them), who are more interested in compiling treatises imitating Latin classics than in giving solid information.

If the wine culture found in books is approximate and tentative, the same does not hold true for cities like Naples, Venice, or Genoa. There, the distribution of wine took place through various centralized bureaucratic offices that mostly regulated wine supplies for the people, all the while keeping a sharp eye out for the products intended for the rich. So in Genoa supplies of ordinary wine for the population were assured either by resorting to wines produced on the Riviera and Corsica or by importing them from France, Spain, and indeed throughout the Mediterranean. Experts were sent to the different countries gather detailed information on the quality and prices for both the better and the ordinary wines.

The wine trade privileged the plains and sea- and riverports because they accommodated the shipping of large casks in sufficient number and capacity to reduce the per-unit price of transportation. The regions squeezed between mountain ranges and hills remained almost isolated until the advent of railroads.

The English and the Dutch took precautions to ensure their provisions of sweet wines. The French, however, who had an adequate supply of sweet wine but also had so many first-class dry red wines, started a little discussed revolution that made the fortune of the wines of Bordeaux and Burgundy, to mention only the best known. From the seventeenth century on but taking hold fully only in the eighteenth, red and white wines of great quality and with nothing fake about their aristocratic breeding were offered for sale. Refined and vinified with care and expertise, they were made to conquer the world, and conquer it they did, remaining dominant and virtually alone on the market for at least a century. Only Andalusia could compete with French wine in offering a high-quality product. The rest of the world lagged behind. The marquis Antinori and a few other aristocrats at Montalcino in Tuscany, the marquise Falletti at Barolo in the Piedmont, the royal holdings of Fontanafredda and Barolo, also in the Piedmont, sent the first bottles of their harvest to market after 1850. Until then the best grapes were vinified sweet and possible fizzy, "scratchy," as one used to say. There is no mystery here for anyone: the oenologists of Montalcino, Barolo, and Fontanafredda were French.

Here too were born the coupling of wines with foods and the tradition of building entire meals around a harmonized sequence of wines. I believe this revolution was the most important event in wine culture in the Early Modern period. A head start of one hundred fifty years had given French wines an enormous advantage compared to the others.

In the last two decades viticulture and vinification have come to life in countries where vines have flourished. But the difference in price of French products steered to market from Bordeaux and Burgundy has signaled a considerable advantage for the French. Nor should one neglect to mention their monopoly of champagne (invented in the early modern for the English market) and of the sweet noble-rot sauternes from the ancient chateau d'Yquem.

The wines of the whole world appeared on the tables and were stored in the wine cellars of the rich. In the eighteenth century the Durazzo of Genoa drank "picolit" from the Friuli, as well as châteaux Lafitte, Ximenez, Graves, and so on.

The same wines, along with château d'Yquem and other great vintages, were found at the end of the seventeenth century and the beginning of the eighteenth in the cellars of many Genoese families, either those living in Genoa itself or those who were transferred to Naples, Salerno (the Imperiale), or Rome (Doria Pamphili). Strong ties with relatives who had become Spanish and the high quality of wines from Jerez de la Frontera completed the richly endowed Genoese cellar with Andalusian wines and some of the best produced in Europe.

Local or regional wines (except for the muscatel from Taggia) were still intended for the masses, for drinking in country houses or in the kitchen. The cellar of an attaché at the embassy in Vienna (1784) contained among others, vino del Capo, Ximenez sherry, madeira, malmsey, Burgundy, Frontignan, Bordeaux, and more. Production centered on fine vintages (*grands crus*) was already the norm in France and Spain in the eighteenth century, while in Italy, with a few exceptions, distinctions of vineyard and estate only came about in the 1970s. As for the peasants' country wine, I discuss it in the chapter devoted to water. The wine called "da bocca," described with the adjective "medium-sweet," in its time remained part of peasant drinking habits. At this point, though, the ruling classes drank French style.

Wine signals the territorial boundaries of a civilization, accompanies food, and enhances its flavors. It is also an officially accepted food and if of good quality a beverage of high prestige (and price), leading to drunkenness only if consumed in excessive quantity. The same holds true for beer. Of course, there were people in Europe, even in the Early Modern period, who preferred drunkenness to the pleasure of wine and used it for hasty binge drinking.

A few words on aquavits: Fernand Braudel writes, "The Dutch made the fortune of all the aquavits beginning in the seventeenth century. These alcohols are for special palates and special tastes. The southern lands look ironically on these drinkers from the north." And sometimes they express a vexation, as exemplified by Baccio Durazzo, writing from Smyrna in 1667: "In the evening there is no one to talk to. The English and Dutch were here but with their way of

FIGURE 49
The Barrel Gives Wine, engraving by Giuseppe Maria Mitelli,
from *Proverbi figurati* (Illustrated proverbs) (Bologna, 1677).

drinking they are soon completely drunk." This annoying drinking habit soon became a commercial opportunity and created demand. In 1664 in Genoa there were forty-one masters in the art of retailing aquavit and at least ten unauthorized. Among the authorized sellers at least one had a Germanic surname. The presence of Dutch boats and of German and English retailers who preferred aquavit to wine increased the demand. In Genoa in 1644 there were more sellers of aquavit than rotisseries or fishmongers. And this doesn't even include the unauthorized sellers found in the back alleys.

Wine jug and basin

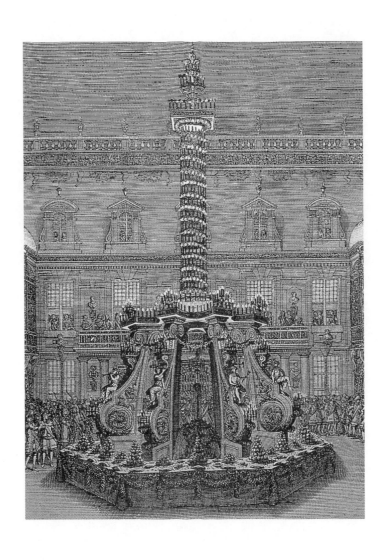

FIGURE 50
Buffet at the court of Versailles, engraving, 1668.

CHAPTER EIGHTEEN

Dining with Discernment

A vast body of writings insists on the elaborately baroque manifestations of Italian cuisine, on banquets that provoke indigestion even in those who merely glance over multiple-course menus of meals fantastic beyond measure. Despite these extravagant descriptions, the foods consumed day by day in the seventeenth and eighteenth centuries by the richest families in Italy (therefore the richest in the world at that time) were not nearly so irrational.

I have collected tens of thousands of daily menus, which I am attempting to arrange in sequence and alphabetically. These cultural materials deal with the great families of Florence, Genoa, Bologna, Naples, Milan, and the like, documenting luxurious habits of dining characterized by the use of local available products (the emphasis is on game in Florence and Rome and more on expensive seafood in Genoa, Naples, and Ferrara). These documents never present the lavish extravagances of princely feasts.

When the research and systematic ordering of available data are finished, I shall gather in one or two volumes the results of this labor. Only then will I be able write with certainty that I found the menus to be pricier (because of the fish) on Fridays and Saturdays, that Carnival and Easter were marked by more lavish feasts than Christmas and New Year's, and that they in turn were surpassed by the feast days of local saints and the almost pagan recurring festivals marking the seasons.

When they were not writing cookbooks, the cooks of the aristocratic families, once outside the noble palazzi, took their savings and set up shop: taverns, inns, drinking houses, or "cooks' shops" (food purveyors).

The trade guild of cooks was in many cities limited to *rotisseurs* (in France *traiteurs*, purveyors of prepared food). These were allowed to practice freely their chosen profession of cooking for the great families. (Who would have had the impudence to inconvenience Lord Farnese, patron of the great cook from Palermo, Carlo Nascia?) They could also continue to work in public eating houses and taverns. But to open up prepared food shops they had to belong to the very restricted guild of cooks. These shops sold prepared foods and furnished catering services for very exacting banquets.

Aristocrats had their cooks in their palazzos, but if, say, the council of notables or the directors of an institution like the Bank San Giorgio decided to dine together in their headquarters several times a year, they hired the registered cook, who, with his helpers, furnished all the necessaries for the kitchen, the crockery and glasses for the table, the tablecloths, and the decorations. He did the shopping and did the cooking. He then presented the bill for the purchases and rental of utensils and collected his salary and that of his assistant. The salaries were surprisingly high, which explains the barriers erected for selective entry into the guild and the exclusionary resistance of those already members. The salaries also reveal the respect and consideration the nobles had for their cooks. "The nobility held their cooks in high esteem [*pretio magno*]," wrote a chronicler at the end of the Middle Ages.

All those who served domestically or in shops, drinking houses, inns, and taverns learned both to prepare food and to

FIGURE 51
Sixteenth-century engraving of Jacopo Bassano's
The Supper at Emmaus.

serve, and it was up to them to preserve the knowledge and the know-how of what we now call traditional cooking.

The great chefs continued to experiment even after the French Revolution, when the bourgeoisie in Paris glorified the new breed of restaurateurs, the former cooks of recently decapitated nobles. The end of the ancien régime quickly had its consequences. The Napoleonic wars brought all the way to Russia young men who did not know what military service really was. Battles and sieges brought hunger even where rulers and governments had for centuries providently been able to avert it. Examples of this can be found in the well-documented siege of Genoa at the time of Masséna and at the end of the Venetian republic, when it was said "the plague raged, we lacked bread, on the bridge the white flag fluttered." This city had never seen such bad times.

So ended the Early Modern period, and so began a tragic road for the people. A succession of ever more frequent and, from the nineteenth century on, ever more deadly wars led to indescribable suffering, criminal nationalism, and destruction on a scale never yet seen. And hunger, this time real hunger, and alcoholism and featureless foods, uniform foods to feed the masses equally (they said): bread and marmalade and a little tea for the victims of the massacre of Manchester described by Ugo Foscolo.

Only after the Second World War did Europeans agree that war was no longer a question of honor and that there was no particular glory in bombing unarmed people from on high. Not everybody understood this, but the suffering and real hunger experienced by civilian populations (not to mention those in concentration camps and gulags) were more real and certainly worse than anything suffered by the populations of the Middle Ages and the Early Modern period.

I do not wish to discuss the values of the new European order. I only want to say that the great revolution has remained unfulfilled in its basic principles and that since

Napoleon there have been two centuries of massacre in Europe, in Africa, and wherever European arms and cannons have reached. All this has been accompanied by two centuries of hunger (for the lower classes), which convinces us that the situation earlier had to have been worse. That isn't true.

Seeing that to shorten my treatise I have left out many things (and goodness knows how many others I have forgotten), I feel exempt from the oversimplifications required by the need to conclude. I close therefore with an observation suggested to me by some cultural debates.

The world of foods requires unobtrusive erudition. It is well known that curiosity is the basic thrust toward knowledge, which in turn is the necessary precondition for pleasure. Knowledge enhances the choice and the quantity of offerings on the market, including the biodiversity of products, favors the exchange of ideas, and stimulates curiosity. So knowledge even in the choice of foods seems fundamental.

We call culture whatever concerns communication: writing, poetry, music, painting, sculpture, architecture (that intended to communicate, such as churches and princely palazzi, not private buildings). Whatever else we do not want within the domain of culture remains and must remain outside.

But cuisine is above all communication. How could we call "Convivio" (with Dante) or "Symposium" (with Plato) pigging out just to fill the belly with food? If cuisine does not belong to culture, why do we have a cuisine of the court and a local cuisine of the *terroir*? I do not dare to answer my own question but content myself with examining the material culture of food, to use an expression that seems coined to satisfy everyone.

Pair of scales

FIGURE 52
Wood engraving from Cristoforo Messisbugo, *Banchetti
compositioni di vivande et apparecchio generale* (Banquets,
foods, equipment, and utensils) (Ferrara, 1549).
(Rome, Collection of the Casanatense Library).

APPENDIX

Dining with Christopher Columbus

The discovery of America on October 12, 1492, signaled an important turning point in world history. The dimensions of the world changed in the minds of politicians, geographers, philosophers, and—slowly, very slowly—in the minds of the common people. Until the first years of the sixteenth century the material existence of the people remained that of the Middle Ages. But the American novelty invaded the cuisine of the elite, who quickly adopted the turkey and cocoa. It took a long time, however, for corn, tomatoes, and potatoes to conquer the kitchen, encroaching via the path of popular culinary habits, which quickly adopted the chili pepper. That fiery fruit could be grown in the garden or in a pot and could replace that expensive condiment pepper.

Columbus spent his youth in Genoa and Savona. Soon he moved to Portugal and then to Spain, where he lived the better (and also the worse) part of his life. He even visited England.

I offer here a short anthology of recipes taken from cookbooks of the aforementioned countries (all reproduced in *Colombo a tavola: Antologia di ricette d'epoca*, ed. Giovanni

Rebora [Savona: Ermes Editoria Comunicazione, 1992]).
Among these, some (in italics in the text) have been
reviewed and modified by Chef Pinin Cipollina in light of
tastes and kitchen utensils that, from the Middle Ages to our
day, have radically changed.

Sliced Eel

Among medieval taste treats, the eel enjoyed great prestige.
Pope Martin IV (Symon de Brie) ended up in Dante's *Purgatory* for indulging this weakness:

> He purged through fasting
> Bolsena eel and Vernaccia wine.

Various recipes exist, but I prefer to transcribe the one
provided by Gentile Sermini in the short story where Signor
Meoccio tells the cook how to prepare a beautiful fat eel:

Here is the treat I saw him make: first peel the eel with
boiling water and remove the insides and chop off tail
and head, then rinse well and chop into even slices of an
inch, more or less. Put these on a spit with sprigs of lau-
rel between the slices, so that the slices don't stick
together. And so roast these on a moderate fire. . . . Put
in a bowl salt, vinegar, and a drop of oil with four spices
inside—that is, pepper, spices, cloves and chopped celery, of each of these a half ounce—and with a small
sprig of rosemary, and when it is well cooked, remove
the juice to a gelatin shell and therein put the thirsty
slices. Then on this put six pomegranates with twenty
oranges and with many fine spices on top of this, then a
hot pan's worth of blood pudding covers this so that it
remains hot until brought to the table.

Dressing for Fish, Ligurian Style
(Also Called Sauce alla Cannellina)

Into the fish kettle put the thoroughly cleaned and washed fish (capon, pullet, scorpion, and other soup ingredients); cover this with a little cold water, and bring this to a boil once or twice to allow it expand and be minced easily into another casserole with olive oil that simmers gently, rosemary, parsley, and chopped spring onions. Cook for around twenty to twenty-five minutes, flavor, stir, and then sift through a fine sieve. Put back on the fire to thicken. Best for dried pasta or Lenten lean foods. Do not add spices to bring out the flavor.

Baby Livers

The following recipe is taken from a cookbook written in Latin by Robert d'Angiò and translated into Italian in the fourteenth century.

Take the liver, cut into pieces, and grill these in a pan; when they are not overcooked, wrap with slabs of pork, and cook. Once cooked, put them in a pot, season as instructed above [see below]; wrapping each liver in the pork slabs individually is better.

The flavoring referred to is the following: "Take spices with saffron and pepper softened with good wine. Pour onto the livers in the pot and cook properly and eat."

Panned Partridge

I do not care to think that Christopher Columbus, who claimed to be very pious, even mystical, ever transgressed the rule of abstinence from meat, and I believe therefore that he fasted on the prescribed days, but I like to imagine that at least on his wedding day (his father-in-law was a dignitary) or at the court in Lisbon the future admiral may have tried some important dishes, perhaps even partridge, a dish certainly well represented in cookbooks and on pottery. The recipe I offer here was translated from the Portuguese.

Take a partridge and lightly roast as though preparing a salmi, then cut into pieces as though to eat it and put into a pot [of terra-cotta; the original text read *tigela*, that is, *tegola*, *teglia*]. Take the partridge and a little sliced onion (the onion should first have been "drowned" in oil and cream). Put the whole into the hot pot with its *adubo* [that is, its "flavoring"; in Ligurian dialect the word *adubo* is still used]: cabbage, pepper, and saffron. The partridge should be coated in flour. Add vinegar diluted with water and half-cover the partridge. Put on the embers to cook and add salt. Remove it.

Partridge in Adubo

Partridge has delicate flesh and is very nutritious. The fully grown bird (more than one year old) is generally a little dry and hard and should be cooked either in a steamed casserole or in a salmi. Baby partridge (under one year) is preferable for roasting. Partridges and baby partridges are dressed with thin strips of bacon.

Clean and turn the partridge, cutting it into quarters, salt, sprinkle with a touch of flour; put it in the casserole (baking pan) with generous amounts of preheated and frothing butter; cover uniformly all sides and flamber with a bit of brandy. Keep warm for a while.

Into the cleaned pan (or another) drown without burning and until clarified a finely sliced white spring onion in butter and cream or, as I prefer, with the finest olive oil.

When the onion mixture is clear (not burned, I repeat), add the lightly browned partridge quarters and its "adubo" flavoring (a mince of celery, carrot, parsley), freshly ground white pepper, a measured dose of salt, and a touch of saffron free-floating in a bit of water or clarified broth. Flavor the hen well under a gentle flame.

Add a generous glass of white vinegar diluted with water, mix in gently, and put the covered pan in a preheated oven at medium heat; let cook for at least thirty to thirty-five minutes.

Arrange the partridge quarters tastefully on a heated platter, surrounding them with slices of toasted, buttered bread; strain the cooked gravy, glaze the aromatic meats, and serve hot, with the sauce well bound in a separate gravy bowl.

Recipe for Rabbit

An animal raised in rural families, rabbit dishes belong to common people's cooking and rarely appear in recipe books. Widespread in Liguria and retailed in cities by poulterers, rabbit probably ended up on the table of the Columbus family. The Portuguese recipe I offer here might have stirred memories in the admiral; one suspects that rabbit was a frequent dish in his father-in-law's house.

Roasted Rabbit. Take a finely chopped onion and cook it in butter or in lard. Then add saffron, pepper, and ginger diluted with vinegar. Put this among the rabbit pieces and bring to a boil, then put some bread slices on a serving platter and serve the rabbit on top of the bread.

Recipe for Lamprey

Lamprey, a fish with great prestige, was always present in Portuguese cooking (from which comes the following recipe), as well as in Galician and Bordelaise cuisine.

Take the lamprey washed in hot water and pull out its insides over a fresh pan in order to collect its blood. Then roll the lamprey in this pan and add coriander, parsley, and finely chopped onion; add a little oil and cover with a lid. When this is well kneaded, add a tiny bit of water and vinegar, pepper, saffron, and a bit of ginger.

Two Vegetable Recipes

In Tuscan recipes of the period, greens and vegetables were not considered worthy of inclusion in culinary publications, but I think artichokes and asparagus (Mediterranean style) should not be forgotten, and I can imagine that Columbus would have appreciated them. Certainly, in the taverns of Seville one might have been served dishes like the two following recipes translated from the Spanish.

ARTICHOKES WITH MEAT

Cut the meat and put it in a pot with water, salt, two spoonfuls of *almori* [a widely known sauce whose exact composition has not reached us], one of vinegar, and another of oil, pepper, and dry coriander. Put on the fire and, when cooked, clean the artichokes, boil them, cut into tiny pieces, and sprinkle on the meat. Raise [the mixture] to the boil; thicken with breadcrumbs and two eggs, and sprinkle with pepper when the mixture has been put on the serving plate.

ASPARAGUS GREENS

Cut the meat into round pieces and put in a pot with a big onion and water, pepper, salt, dried coriander, two spoonfuls of *almori*, and as much again of fine oil. Put on the fire and, when the meat is ready, cut boiled asparagus, mince them, and put them on the meat. Thicken with egg yolk.

Lamb with Truffles

I include another Spanish recipe, this one based on meat and black truffles.

Cut the meat into tiny pieces and boil in water with onions, salt, and pepper, and when the salt and water have boiled away throw washed sliced truffles into the pot, and when the truffles are ready bathe the pot with a little *almori*, after having stirred in as many eggs as you like. Sprinkle with cinnamon and powdered rue.

Panada of Meat or Fish

This translation, like the others, follows the path of the original recipe (included in *The Cook's Book*, by Rupert de Nola, published for the first time in Catalan at the time of Columbus). One is advised to read it carefully because the sequence of operations can be confusing. When Nola writes that one should "put the meat or fish . . . ," he forgets to say where (in a thin sauce). The author also resumes his instructions on how to prepare the panada after having directed that it be "put in the oven."

> Boil the meat or fish (if meat, boil it some more). When thoroughly boiled, take off the fire and put into cold water, then make the panada (that is, prepare the layer dough in the pan, put in the meat or fish cut into small pieces, cover with a sheet of dough, and put in the oven, but leave opening holes in the cover so it can breathe, otherwise it might break in the oven [*sclataria*, a vestige of southern dialects using the verb *schiattare*, to burst). Put the meat into the panada with fine sauce.
>
> If fish, more pepper; if meat, more salt. Shortly before removing it from the oven push into the holes an egg vigorously beaten in a bowl with bitters or else with orange juice or good white vinegar, then put it back into the oven the length of an "Our Father" and an "Ave Maria," then serve.

Two Fish Recipes

I offer two more Catalan recipes based on fish.

A GOOD SAUCE FOR A MEDIUM-SIZED FISH
TO BE PUT IN THE OVEN

If you want to make a good sauce for a medium-size fish that is going into the oven, take two or three bulbs of garlic and two or three walnuts, and grind them well together. Take some toasted bread dipped in vinegar, put it into the mortar, and grind the whole well. Then take some well-grated spices and add them; add cold water so that the sauce is not too thick. Put the fish into a casserole and take parsley and sage and chop them fine to sprinkle on the fish. Add the sauce and a little oil.

SALMON IN CASSEROLE

Take the salmon and clean it thoroughly. Then put the salmon into a casserole with spices, that is, a bit of pepper, ginger, and saffron. Grind this well and sprinkle on the fish with salt, some bitter or orange juice, and put it on a good fire, over sustained heat. Then take white almonds, raisins, pine nuts, and all the herbs, that is, marjoram, parsley, and mint. When the stew is more than half-cooked, put it all into the casserole, and it is ready.

Marzipan

Marzipan is just one example of the many products and terms imported from other cultures. The *marzapane*, from the Arabic *marzaban*, was a unit of measure used in Cyprus and Armenia as a submultiple of *modius*. As was the case for *amphora*, *jar*, and *barrel*, the unit of measure eventually lent its name to the wrapping, to the container, which at least at its origins was calibrated according to the measure itself. The *marzapane* was a light wooden box, made of a wood similar to that used for sieves. Its shape was oval, and it had a cover made of the same wood. The box was used to ship sweets made with flour, almond paste, and other ingredients to Cyprus. Given that these sweets took on the shape of the box and resembled bread, the name of the envelope or wrapper was soon transferred to the contents, which were then called *marzapane*, or marzipan.

Already in the fourteenth century Balducci Pegolotti, compiler of a business guide, sought to distinguish the box from its contents, referring to "weight and cost of wooden box into which you put the marzipan when it is fresh." A few lines later he specified: "[it] is for the wood alone, without the edible marzipan."

The boxes continued to be called *marʒapani* and were used to store correspondence and important documents; thus the expression *aprire i marʒapani* (to open the marzipan), in the sense of disclosing (embarrassing) secrets. Here is a recipe from the end of the fifteenth century:

Peel the almonds thoroughly. Crush them with a pestle as much as possible so they don't have to be put through the grinder. To make these almonds whiter, tastier, and sweeter to the mouth, soften them in cool water for a day and a night and even more. And crush them along with a little rosewater so they don't get oily. And if you want to make the aforementioned torte good put into it equal measures of sugar, of ground almonds, that is, a pound of one and the other or more or less as you like, and put in another ounce or two of good rosewater, and mix all these together thoroughly. Then take the cornets of sugar and bathe first with rosewater; spread on the bottom of the pan and into them put the mixture. Put it to cook in an oven or on a fire like other tortes, taking care to use a gentle flame and to check often, so that it doesn't burn. Remember that marzipan tortes should be light and small, not thick and heavy.

The bibliography dealing with culinary history grows from month to month: the topic is fashionable and could lead to the creation of a culinary cookbook award. Those who want to be informed or to research in depth specific topics will soon find themselves drowning in a sea of "titleography," writings put together especially for university competitive examinations. It is therefore no easy task to choose from among the thousands of titles produced by authors wanting to show off their learning but mostly too respectful of previously acquired knowledge and of earlier writings—in short, devoted to clichés.

Food: A Culinary History, ed. Jean-Louis Flandrin and Massimo Montanari, trans. ed. Albert Sonnenfeld (New York: Columbia University Press, 1999) offers a series of highly interesting studies, extended and sustained by essential bibliography. The authors who contributed to the volume are wholly qualified, and their resumés include well-known and original publications based on documented research and vast bibliographical inquiry, either in book form or scattered (unfortunately) in a host of specialized periodicals. Jean-Louis Flandrin can claim publications of the first order both for the medieval and Early Modern periods (he edited, among others, *Le cuisinier françois* [Paris: Montalba, 1983]). From the bibliography cited in footnotes one can trace his learned society papers in order to find out more about his vast scholarly production. Massimo Montanari has devoted himself especially to the Middle Ages.

In particular, see Jean-Louis Flandrin, "Les pâtes dans la cuisine provençale" (Pasta in Provençal cuisine), *Médiévales: Langue, Textes, Histoire*, nos. 16–17 (1989): 65–75. See also, on pages 61 through 64 of the same issue, Massimo Montanari, "Notes sur l'histoire des pâtes en Italie" (Notes on the history of pasta in Italy), as well as other very interesting contributions. In issue number 5 of *Médiévales: Langue, Textes, Histoire*, published in 1983, on pages 5 through 15, see Flandrin's "Brouet, potages, bouillons" (Gruel, soups, bouillons).

Montanari has published articles in many reviews. I don't think I'm allowing the friendship that ties us to cloud my vision when I say that the three volumes of *Nuovo convivio: Storia e cultura dei piaceri della tavola in età moderna* (New banquet: History and culture of the pleasures of the table in the Early Modern period) (Rome-Bari: Laterza, 1991) belong to the best traditions of culinary history. To these three volumes I would add *La fame e l'abbondanza* (Hunger and abundance), also published by Laterza, in 1993.

Among the authors in the major volumes edited by Flandrin and Montanari I mention only two (with apologies to the others): Alberto Capatti, who wrote about the taste for preserved foods, venturing down an important path, if one littered with risks (of cliché), to produce a reasonable and rational history of the last two hundred years. In addition, of great interest for northern Europe is the article by Michel Morineau.

For this book I have above all used archival documents, including those brought to light by my collaborators. See, for example, N. Calleri, *L'arte dei formaggiai a Genova tra Quattro e Cinquecento* (The art of cheesemaking in Genoa between the fifteenth and sixteenth centuries) (Genoa, 1996), a volume published on behalf of the Department of Modern and Contemporary History of the University of Genoa. Calleri also has in print an article entitled "All About Cooks" in which he surveys rotisseries. He is researching tuna and tuna-fishing equipment and industry at the behest of François Doumenge, director of the Oceanographic Museum of Monaco. See also F. Ciciliot and E. Riccardi, *Archeologia dell'acciuga* (Archaeology of the anchovy) (Vado Ligure: CSAM, 1998).

For cheeses, see I. Naso, *Formaggi nel medioevo* (Cheeses in the Middle Ages) (Turin: Segnalibro, 1990). I got information on greens from C. Riccobene, "Ortolani e revenditori di frutta a Genova tra il XV e il XVIII secolo" (Kitchen gardeners and fruit retailers in Genoa between the fifteenth and eighteenth centuries), *La Berio* (Genoa), no. 2 (1993). On the supply of meat, I took advantage of three volumes in which G. Puppo has gathered the greater part of the available documentation on the topic from Piedmont, Piacenza, Cremona, and Genoa: "L'approvvigionamento della carne a Genova nel XVIII secolo" (Meat supplies and suppliers in Genoa in the eighteenth century), thesis for the Laurea degree, University of Genoa, 1992–93; "Le carni piemontesi a Genova nel XVIII secolo" (Piedmontese meats in Genoa in the eighteenth century), in *Greggi mandrie e pastori nelle Alpi occidentali* (Flocks, cattle ranches, cowherds in the western Alps), ed. R. Comba, A. Del Verme, and I. Naso (Cuneo-Rocca de' Baldi: Società per gli studi storici, archeologici ed artistici della provincia di Cuneo, 1996); and "L'approvvigionamento della carne a Genova nel XVIII secolo" (Meat supplies in Genoa in the eighteenth century), *La Berio*, no. 1 (1994).

As for the consumption of food, C. Flammia, G. Villa, R. Villa (Cerretto Prize 1998), and B. Giuliani are to be praised for their impressive collection of documents located in private archives in Genoa, Florence, Rome, and Naples, not to mention the archives of food consumption in Paris and those at the convent of San Gerolamo of Cornigliano. These are currently being prepared and will soon be published.

I have turned to the very learned and entertaining volume by F. Portinari, *Il piacere della gola* (The pleasures of gluttony) (Milan: Camunia, 1986). I have also had recourse to many works by P. Camporesi, such as *La terra e la luna* (Earth and moon) (Milan, 1989), rich in facts on the royal cuisine and in sharp analyses; *Il pane selvaggio* (Primitive bread) (Bologna: Mulino, 1983); *Il paese della fame* (The land of hunger) (Bologna: Mulino, 1985; *La carne impossibile* (The impossible meat) (Milan: Saggiatore, 1983); *Mito gastronomico e verità alimentare* (Gastronomic myth and nutritional truth), in *L'Emilia Romagna* (Milan, 1974); and *Il brodo indiano* (Indian brew) (Milan: Garzani, 1990).

For chocolate (Indian brew), also see the entertaining book by Sophie D. Coe and Michael D. Coe, *The True Story of Chocolate* (New York: Thames and Hudson, 1996); under the imprint of the editor Rosellina Archinto, there has appeared a delicious little book, A. Dumas, *Lettere sulla cucina a un sedicente buongustaio napoletano* (Letters on cuisine to a would-be gourmet in Naples), in which the author of *The Three Musketeers* offers precious information on the North African ways of roasting mutton. For salt, see J.-C. Hocquet, *Il sale e il potere* (Salt and power) (Ecig. Genoa, 1990).

Among the contributions cited are G. Doria, *Uomini e terre di un borgo collinare* (Men and lands of a hill-town) (Milan: Giuffrè, 1968), and Marvin Harris, *Good to Eat: Riddles of Food and Culture* (New York: Simon and Schuster, 1985), in which one finds interesting suggestions. The spice market of the Middle Ages has been studied by M. Balard, and the same Balard studied manuscripts dealing with German cuisine, a theme infrequently studied outside of the Germanic world. For spices, also consult C. M.

Cipolla, *Allegro ma non troppo* (Bologna: Mulino, 1988). On the consumption of dried pasta in Naples, see E. Sereni, "I napoletani: Da mangiafoglia a mangiamaccheroni" (The Neapolitans: From leaf eaters to macaroni eaters), in *Terra nuova e buoi rossi* (New land and red beef) (Turin: Einaudi, 1981).

For citrus and Mediterranean fruit shipped to northern Europe, see A. Bicci, "Frutti mediterranei e grano del Baltico nel secolo degli olandesi" (Mediterranean fruit and Baltic grain in the Dutch century), in *La storia dei Genovesi: Atti del convegno di studi sui ceti dirigenti nelle istituzioni della Repubblia di Genova* (Genoa, 1986). For products originating in America, see C. Maccagni, "Alimentari e farmaci dal Nuovo Mondo" (Foods and drugs from the New World), *Minerva Pediatrica* 39, no. 21 (1997).

Very interesting are the following: A. Meiji De Pardo, *El comercio del Bacalo en la Galicia del XVIII* (The cod trade in Galicia in the eighteenth century) (La Coruña, 1980), and J. Leonartt and J. Ma. Camarassa, *La pesca a Catalunya el 1722, segons un manuscrit de Joan Salvador I Riera* (Fishing in Catalonia in 1722, according to a manuscript by Juan Salvador I Riera) (Barcelona: Museo Maritim, 1987).

For the potato, I have referred to the *Pratica Agraria* by Giovanni Battarra from Rimini, published for the first time in 1778 (see Montanari, *Nuovo Convivio*, pp. 341–45). For the consumption of various foods, see L. Tagliaferri, *La magnificenza privata* (Private opulence) (Genoa: Marietti, 1995).

For a few details on Naples, see M. Leone, *La vita quotidiana a Napoli ai tempi di Masaniello* (Daily life in Naples in the time of Masaniello) (Milan: Rizzoli, 1994). For Sicily, see O. Cancila, *Aspetti di un mercato siciliano* (Aspects of a Sicilian marketplace) (Rome-Bari: Laterza, 1980; reprint, Palermo: Palumbo, 1993). By the same author, see *L'economia della Sicilia: Aspetti storici* (The economy of Sicily: Historical aspects) (Milan: Saggiatore, 1992) and *Baroni e popolo nella Sicilia del grano* (Barons and commoners in grain-growing Sicily) (Palermo: Palumbo, 1983).

On the problems of the population, see M. Livi Bacci, *Populazione e alimentazione: Saggio sulla storia demografica europea* (Populations and foods: Essay on European demographic history) (Bologna: Mulino, 1987).

Finally, one must not fail to consider the trilogy by F. Braudel: *Civiltà materiale, economia e capitalismo (secoli XV–XVIII)* (Material civilization, economy, and capitalism [fifteenth through eighteenth centuries]) (Turin: Einaudi, 1981–82), especially the first volume, *Le strutture del quotidiano* (The structures of daily life).

Iron for pasta

INDEX

Venice: colonies of (*continued*)
spices and, 104, 105; and
sugar trade, 94; tableware
of, 144; war and, 166; and
wine, 155, 157
Vernaccia wine, 155
vinello/vinetta, 32
Voltaire, 61

walnuts, 93
war: and cheese production,
38; feeding prisoners, 122;
feeding the troops, 80, 81,
154; and food supplies,
111–12; herring and, 72;
leather production and, 51;
and protein acquisition,
127; and suffering, 166–67
water, 24–35, 31–32
wealth: colonization and,
136–38; measurement of,
20, 59, 60; menus and,

163–64; tableware artisans
and, 146. *See also* class;
poverty; (the) superfluous
wheel, 134, 139
white bread, 4
wine: the Americas and, 132,
136; class and consumption
of, 153–55, 157, 158, 159;
drunkenness, 159, 161; with
food, 149, 158; fragmentation of farms and, 6; Greek-
style, 154, 155; names of,
155, 157; peasants and, 32,
155, 159; pouches for,
49–50; production of, 32,
153–55, 157–58, 159; trade
in, 155, 157–59, 161; transportation of, 49–50, 136,
155, 157
wool production, 48, 49

zucchini, 120